A POSTSCRIPT Cookbook

A POSTSCRIPT Cookbook

Barry Thomas

VNR VAN NOSTRAND REINHOLD
New York

First published 1988

Published by
MACMILLAN EDUCATION LTD
Houndmills, Basingstoke, Hampshire RG21 2XS
and London
Companies and representatives
throughout the world

Printed in Great Britain by
The Camelot Press Ltd., Southampton

Published in North America by
Van Nostrand Reinhold
115 Fifth Avenue, New York, NY 10003 USA.

ISBN 0–442–23686–7
Library of Congress 88–27995

Compaq is a trademark of Compaq Computer Systems
IBM is a registered trademark of International Business Machines Incorporated
Linotronic 300 is a registered trademark of Allied Corporation
Macintosh is a trademark of Apple Computer Incorporated
PostScript is a trademark of Adobe Systems Incorporated
Times and Helvetica are registered trademarks of Allied Corporation
Ventura Publisher is a trademark of Ventura Software Incorporated
WordStar is a registered trademark of MicroPro International Corporation

CONTENTS

PREFACE

As with all computer hardware, the development of printing technology has come on apace in the last couple of years. Doubtless it will continue to do so. The most recent and most impressive developments in this field have been in the area of laser and LED page printers.

Now that the price of these printers is within the range of more and more people, there are more and more people who want to make the most of this affordable new technology. That's what this book is all about.

Computer technology develops at an increasingly dramatic rate, daring us to find new ways to put it to use. But as a result of the sheer speed at which the new developments become widely available, the number of people who are able to wring the last ounce of usefulness out of them is smaller and smaller.

This book is intended to help you realise more of the potential of your POSTSCRIPT printer. The power of POSTSCRIPT is limited only by your imagination. Just about any image that can be printed on paper can be produced by POSTSCRIPT.

Many people shy away from the 'awesome' task of actually programming – whatever the language. This book is not intended as a full tutorial in programming in general or POSTSCRIPT programming in particular, but it IS intended to show that even very short and simple POSTSCRIPT programs can make your printer really earn its keep.

This book contains programs which produce many different styles of text and just as many styles of graphics. It even contains programs which will expand the number of typefaces your printer can produce.

This book was originated on a POSTSCRIPT laser printer; all of the graphics are taken directly from POSTSCRIPT output and this is still only a fraction of what POSTSCRIPT can do. Now it's over to you.

My thanks must go to Max and Carl Phillips of Strange Software Limited, London, EC1, for their Grabit software which produced the POSTSCRIPT program for the image of the Psion Chess program on page 33. Thanks go also to Iain Janes and Philip Mattimoe of Lotus Reprographic Services Limited, London, W6, who provided plentiful advice and information on POSTSCRIPT typesetting.

This book is for my Marvel of Peru, Fiona Maclean.

1. ALL ABOUT POSTSCRIPT

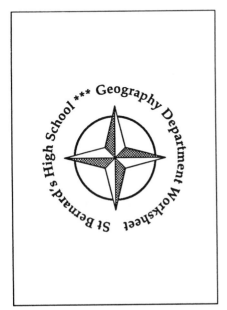

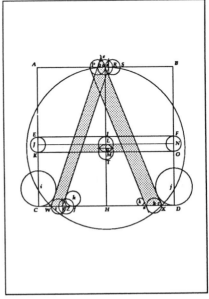

WHAT IS POSTSCRIPT?

The desk-top-publishing revolution is upon us. Usually referred to as DTP, this combination of computing, graphic design, typography and printing is hyped and talked about wherever computers are to be found.

The basic tenet of the DTP school of thought is that anyone can sit at a computer attached to a laser printer and, with the aid of appropriate software, they can design, write, typeset and print their own 'publications'. This book is not designed to argue the case for DTP or that every computer user can overnight become a publishing mogul. It is, however, designed to show the power and flexibility of just one of the links in the DTP chain: POSTSCRIPT.

Many of the DTP software packages and print devices (from laser printers to typesetting machinery costing hundreds of thousands of pounds) understand the document description language POSTSCRIPT. This is a language designed specifically so that one page or a whole complex document containing both text and graphics may be 'described' to the output device in device-independent terms. So the same document description may be given to a (relatively) cheap laser printer as to an expensive typesetting machine and approximately the same document will be produced. The difference is that the version from the typesetting machine will be produced at higher resolution than that from the laser printer.

In each case the document description, i.e. the program, is the same. And if a laser printer is launched tomorrow for half the price of the old models and with twice the resolution, so long as it has POSTSCRIPT it will work in exactly the same way, and your programs will be able to drive it in just the same way as they did the old machine.

THE LANGUAGE

POSTSCRIPT is most like the programming language FORTH. It uses stacks, user defined procedures and postfix notation. It has over 250 operators which cover advanced text handling, graphics and all of the facilities of a general programming language.

The Stack

POSTSCRIPT uses variables for number and text handling just like other languages but it also has a user stack. This is a general purpose object handler which can be used to temporarily hold numbers, strings, arrays, dictionaries, boolean flags, fonts or almost any of the objects which make up the language. The stack is a last-in-first-out (lifo) structure.

Postfix Notation

POSTSCRIPT uses postfix notation, unlike some other languages, for example BASIC, which uses infix notation. Infix notation looks like this:

```
(6 + 4) * 2
```

giving a result of 20. The equivalent statement in postfix notation looks like this:

```
6 4 + 2 *
```

or:

```
2 6 4 + *
```

And there are still other ways of expressing the same statement. The result meanwhile stays on the stack where it can be left until needed or removed and used.

In POSTSCRIPT, the arithmetic operators appear in text form rather than in the usual +, -, /, * format. So the last example shown above would read:

```
2 6 4 add mul
```

The four basic operators are **add, div, mul** and **sub**. The use of these will be described in full later in this book.

The POSTSCRIPT operators, as shall be seen in later chapters, deal with, among other things, colors, miters and shades of gray. In the interests of consistency, the American spelling of these words has been used throughout this book.

User Procedures

Any operator which does not exist in the language but which you might find useful, can be built up from combinations of other operators. These procedures can then be used as if they were resident features of the language. POSTSCRIPT is an interpreted, rather than a compiled, language. However, a facility exists to let your procedures be 'bound', in order to increase running speed if they are used often in a program. The process of binding procedures is rather like compiling in other languages.

USER AND DEVICE SPACE

POSTSCRIPT operates on a plane which is described in terms of the usual mathematical x and and y axes. This plane is referred to as user space, because that is where the user describes, by a series of POSTSCRIPT commands, the text and graphics to be printed.

Device space is dependent upon the internal coordinate system employed by each type of POSTSCRIPT output device to address the points on a page. This space will differ from device to device.

PATHS

A path is a sequence of points which may or may not all be connected. These points describe shapes and the position of the shapes in user space. A path may describe graphics or text or both. There is no restriction on the mixing of text and graphics within a single path.

A path is built up by use of the path operators. These are POSTSCRIPT operators which define parts of a path. The act of describing a path does not make any mark on the page. When a path has been described, there are three options:

1. Stroke the path

To stroke a path means to render an image of the path, which exists in user space, into the device space. Once there it can be physically printed onto a sheet of paper.

2. Fill the path

To fill a path means to paint over the area which the path encloses. This filled path may then be printed onto a sheet of paper.

3. Use the path as a clipping path

A path may be used like a stencil, through which other shapes may be drawn, but excluding certain areas of the page. Any existing path may be made a clipping path.

POSTSCRIPT PROGRAMS

POSTSCRIPT programs can be produced using any word processor with a plain-text (ASCII) facility, or any ASCII text editor. All POSTSCRIPT operators and language elements are handled as straight ASCII text and are sent to a POSTSCRIPT device in this format. This means that they can easily be transferred from machine to machine and transmitted by even quite unsophisticated data-communications systems.

Program Comments

The programs listed in this book are all described in some detail, but they also have embedded comments. Like other languages, POSTSCRIPT programs benefit from the addition of meaningful, explanatory comments. You may understand the flow of your program when you write it, but come back to a program after some months away and it may not be as easy to follow as you had thought!

Comments are preceded by a % character. Any text following a % is ignored up to the end of the line.

Program Structure

It is not the purpose of this book either to provide a full tutorial in the use of POSTSCRIPT, or to teach you how to program. However, the following notes may prove useful in interpreting the program listings included in the following chapters:

- All operators and font names should be typed exactly as they appear in the book, taking note of any upper case letters

- Program lines which contain just numbers simply place those numbers on the stack

- The '/' character starts a definition, either of a font description or a user variable or procedure

- Procedure code is included between braces { } and followed by the **def** operator

- Text strings are included between parentheses ( )

2. USING TEXT

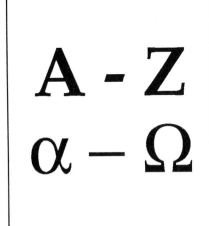

This chapter includes a number of programs which manipulate and print text. The programs may be used as they appear here, or may be adapted to produce the type of output you require. Each program includes embedded comments to explain the program's structure. For further details of any of the operators used, refer to chapter 5 where all of the POSTSCRIPT operators and their syntax are described.

Some of the techniques used in these programs can be combined with others to produce different output. For example, the method of producing gray text may be combined with the program which justifies a body of text.

The programs included in this chapter have been written with an A4 laser printer in mind as the target device. They will, however, work with most POSTSCRIPT devices. If you intend to produce output on any other device, take care to follow any device-dependent procedures required by that device. See also Appendix A on POSTSCRIPT Typesetting.

As you type in these programs, you are recommended to type in the comments, i.e. any text including and following a % character. Also, when you write your own programs it is strongly recommended that you annotate each line with a meaningful comment. This makes the process of deciphering your own programs dramatically easier later on.

SIMPLE TEXT

Helvetica
Times-Roman

Helvetica-Squash
Times-Roman-Squash

This program demonstrates the process of selecting a font, scaling to a chosen size, positioning the current point prior to printing text and, finally, compressing the x axis to produce horizontally compressed text.

To use text, you must select a typeface from the range available on your printer, select a point size (type size is specified in points; 72 points = one inch) and position the current point in user space just where you want your text to appear.

By compressing or expanding one typeface, you can increase the usefulness of a machine which has a limited number of typefaces. For example, by compressing Helvetica to approximately 82% of its usual width, you can produce a very respectable Helvetica Narrow lookalike.

```
% Squashed Typefaces

/squash
{
 /comp exch def              % get x compression factor from stack
 /points exch def            % get point size from stack
 /margin exch def            % get left margin width from stack
 /ypos exch def              % get starting y position from stack

 /newline                    % define newline procedure
 {
  /ypos                      % redefine y position variable
  ypos                       %       for position of next line
  points 1.1 mul sub         % inter-line space is 10% point size
  def
  margin ypos moveto         % move to new y position at margin
 } def

 /helv
 {
  /Helvetica findfont        % select Helvetica
  points scalefont           % set point size
  setfont
 } def

 /times
 {
  /Times-Roman findfont      % select Times
  points scalefont           % set point size
  setfont
 } def

 newline                     % set up start position
 helv                        % select Helvetica
 (Helvetica) show            % show full width string
 newline                     % move down and back to margin
 times                       % select Times
 (Times-Roman) show          % show full width string
 newline                     % move down and back to margin

 comp 1 scale                % scale x axis down

 /margin                     % reset margin to
 margin 1 comp div mul       %    compensate for scaling
```

```
def

    newline                 % insert a blank line gap
    helv                    % select Helvetica
    (Helvetica-Squash) show % show compressed string
    newline                 % move down and back to margin
    times                   % select Times
    (Times-Roman-Squash) show % show compressed string
    newline                 % move down and back to margin
} def

650                         % y position value
50                          % left margin value
64                          % point size
0.82                        % x axis compression factor

squash
showpage                    % print page
```

The program begins by assigning variables for the starting y position, the point size, left margin and a compression factor. As stated above, a compression factor of 0.82 turns Helvetica into an attractive font very much like Helvetica Narrow.

The reverse effect is also possible. Giving a compression factor greater than 1 will expand a font in the x axis. Experiment with different values and see how the text is affected.

Note that when the x axis is compressed or expanded, more or less text will fit across the width of the page, so you may want to change your margins accordingly.

The procedure **newline** performs a carriage return/line feed effect. The current y position is moved down and the current x position returned to the margin. The next procedure, **helv**, selects the font Helvetica and scales it to the point size given at the start of the program. The procedure **times** does the same job for Times-Roman.

Note that the capitals in all font names and the absence of capitals in operators are significant. Using any mixture of upper and lower case other than those given will lead to an error and the program will not operate correctly.

The strings 'Helvetica' and 'Times-Roman' are printed full width, with a newline in between. These are followed by a blank line. The x axis is then scaled to produce compressed text. The next two strings have a tighter feel than the full width fonts. Note also that the ratio of stroke width changes according to the amount of compression (or expansion) you specify. In the example above, the vertical strokes are now only 82% of the thickness of the equivalent horizontal strokes.

GRAY, OUTLINE AND CLIPPED TEXT

This program demonstrates the use of the **setgray** operator to specify gray print and the **charpath** operator to create a path which takes the shape of the outline of a text string. Such an outline is used first to simply stroke onto the page, producing an outline of the current font. An outline is then used as a clipping path, allowing graphics to be clipped to the shape of a text string.

The shades of gray produced by POSTSCRIPT are determined by the operand of the **setgray** operator. Any decimal value between 0 and 1 may be specified. For example:

Operand	Result
0	Black
0.25	Dark Gray
0.5	Mid Gray
0.75	Light Gray
1	White

```
% Fancy Text

/fancy
{
  650                        % get y position from stack
  72                         % get left margin from stack
  100                        % get point size from stack

  /points exch def          % get point size from stack
  /margin exch def          % get margin width from stack
  /ypos exch def            % get start y position from stack
  /xpos margin def          % define variable used in lines proc

  /newline                  % newline procedure
  {
   /ypos                    % redefine y position
   ypos points 1.1 mul sub % spacing is 10% of point size
   def
   margin ypos moveto       % move to new y posn at margin
  } def

  /lines                    % lines procedure
  {
   newpath                  % new path for clipped lines
   0 5 500                  % for 0 to 500 step 5
   {
    ypos points 2 div sub  % start position of line
    moveto
    xpos ypos points add
    lineto                  % end position of line
    /xpos xpos 5 add def    % move across for next line
   } for                    % end of for loop
   stroke                   % stroke lines onto page
  } def

  /gray
```

```
{
  0.8 setgray show 0 setgray  % set gray level, show text
} def                        %    and reset gray level to black

/outlined
{
  true charpath             % set path to outline
} def                       %    of text

/Times-BoldItalic findfont  % select Times
points scalefont            % set point size
setfont

newline                     % reset start position
(Grey Text) gray            % and show gray text

newpath newline             % new path for outline text
(Outline) outlined          % make path of outline
stroke closepath            % stroke text and close path

newpath newline             % new path for clipping path
(Clipped) outlined          % make path of text outline
clip                        % clip to current path
lines closepath             % draw lines and clip them

} def

fancy
showpage                    % print page
```

The important procedures defined in this program are **gray** and **outlined**. The procedure **gray** is used to set the current gray level to a light shade of gray. The procedure **outlined** is used to create a path which takes the form of the outline of a text string.

The program starts with values and variables for the initial y position, margin and point size. These are followed by procedures for carriage return/line feed (**newline**) and a pattern of lines to be clipped in the third part of the program.

Times is selected and scaled to the specified point size. In **gray**, a value of 0.8 is given for the **setgray** operator which gives all subsequent output a light shade of gray. The string Gray Text is printed and the gray level is reset to 0 (black) for subsequent output.

The next procedure, **outlined,** uses the **charpath** operator to produce a path which takes the form of the outline of the characters in the given string. This path behaves just as if you had produced it with the graphics operators **lineto, curveto, arc** and so on. The first outline path is simply stroked onto the page, giving an outline version of the current font. The width of the line is the default line width for the target device.

The second use of **outlined** uses the **clip** operator to produce a clipping path conforming to the shape of the characters in the string. The procedure **lines** is then called to produce a pattern of sloping lines over the top of the string. Only those parts of the lines which lie within the clipping path of the characters are shown when the page is printed.

A clipping path produced in this way can even be used to clip areas of subsequent text, but note that using any clipping path, especially when followed by other complex output may be quite time consuming due to the amount of processing being carried out by the POSTSCRIPT interpreter.

LEFT ALIGNED TEXT

As I walked through the wilderness of this world, I lighted on a certain place, where was a den; and I laid me down in that place to sleep: and as I slept I dreamed a dream. I dreamed, and behold I saw a man clothed with rags, standing in a certain place, with his face from his own house, a book in his hand, and a great burden upon his back. I looked, and saw him open the book, and read therein; and as he read, he wept and trembled: and not being able longer to contain, he brake out with a lamentable cry; saying, 'What shall I do?'

The Pilgrim's Progress, John Bunyan

Prophet of God, in quest of the uttermost, long have you searched the distances for your ship. And now your ship has come, and you must needs go.

The Prophet, Kahlil Gibran.

This program demonstrates the use of the **search** operator for searching one string for another given substring, and the **loop** operator for creating a looping structure which is repeated until explicitly halted by the **exit** operator.

The program takes a text string and prints it left aligned, from a given margin, not exceeding a given line length, breaking the text where necessary to keep the text within the stated limits. The program treats the given string as one paragraph. Paragraph breaks are not catered for.

If the text falls to within 50 points of the bottom of the A4 page, the current page is printed out and a new one started from the same starting position as the first.

```
%   Left aligned text

/leftalign
{
  /points exch def          % get point size
  /margin exch def          % get left margin
  /llength exch def         % get line length
  /ypos exch def            % get initial y position
  /ycur ypos def            % define current y position
  /leading                  % set leading at 2 points
  points 2 add              %   greater than point size
  def

  /Times-Roman findfont     % select Times
  points scalefont setfont  % set point size

  /newline                  % proc for line break
  {                         % proc start
   /ycur                    % drop y position by leading
   ycur leading sub
   def
   margin ycur              % move down and back to margin
   moveto
   ycur 50 lt               % ypos within 50 pts of page end?
   {
     /ycur ypos def         % if so, reset current position
     showpage               %     print current page
     margin ycur moveto     %     and move to page head
   } if
  } def                     % end of newline proc

  margin ypos moveto % move to start point

  {                         % for all text
    ( ) search              % search for a space
    {                       % if found...
     dup stringwidth        % get length of pre space string
     pop currentpoint pop   % get current point
     add llength margin add gt    % will word cross margin?
     {newline} if           % yes, then newline
     show show              % show word and space
    }
    {exit} ifelse           % no space found
  } loop
```

```
    dup stringwidth          % get length of pre space string
    pop currentpoint pop     % get current point
    add llength margin add gt% will word cross margin?
    {newline} if             % yes, then newline
    show                     % show final part of string
} def

(As I walked through the wilderness of this world, \
I lighted on a certain place, where was a den; \
and I laid me down in that place to sleep: and as I \
slept I dreamed a dream. I dreamed, and behold I saw \
a man clothed with rags, standing in a certain place, with \
his face from his own house, a book in his hand, and a \
great burden upon his back. I looked, and saw him open the \
book, and read therein; and as he read, he wept and \
trembled: and not being able longer to contain, he brake \
out with a lamentable cry; saying, 'What shall I do?')

750                        % y start position
450                        % line length
75                         % left margin
32                         % point size


leftalign
newline
newline
/Times-Italic findfont     % select font and print credit
points 0.75 mul scalefont setfont
(The Pilgrim's Progress, John Bunyan) show

showpage
```

The program starts by taking the text to be printed, the starting y position, the line length, left margin and point size from the stack. From the last of these is calculated the inter-line spacing. The text to be printed is in the form of a single string which has been broken into several parts for readability. POSTSCRIPT allows strings to be broken in this way by ending each line with a backslash character (\). When a backslash is followed by a newline character, both are ignored so the newline character is not included as part of the string.

Like in the previous program, the newline procedure performs a carriage return/line feed operation, but this version of newline is rather more sophisticated than the previous one. It checks after each newline to see if the new y position is within 50 points of the bottom of the A4 page. If so, the current page is printed out and a new one started from the same initial point as the first.

Times is selected and scaled to the given point size. Then comes the routine which breaks the text at the appropriate point on each line. This routine is repeated until no further spaces are found in the given string. The routine searches for a space (ASCII 32). The **search** operator returns a true flag when a space is found, and the post match string, the space and the pre match string. These are all placed on the stack.

The routine then checks to see if the word before the space can be fitted on the current line without exceeding the stated line length. If so, the word is printed. If not, a newline is performed and the word is added to the start of the next line. This process is repeated until no spaces are left in the string. At this point, the **exit** operator breaks the loop. Program execution carries on after the **loop** operator. The tail end of the string is checked for size and, if it will fit inside the current line, printed.

Then follows a blank line and the credit and the page is printed out.

JUSTIFIED TEXT

As I walked through the wilderness of this world, I lighted on a certain place, where was a den; and I laid me down in that place to sleep: and as I slept I dreamed a dream. I dreamed, and behold I saw a man clothed with rags, standing in a certain place, with his face from his own house, a book in his hand, and a great burden upon his back. I looked, and saw him open the book, and read therein; and as he read, he wept and trembled: and not being able longer to contain, he brake out with a lamentable cry; saying, 'What shall I do?'

The Pilgrim's Progress, John Bunyan

Prophet of God, in quest of the uttermost, long have you searched the distances for your ship. And now your ship has come, and you must needs go.

The Prophet, Kahlil Gibran

This program demonstrates some of POSTSCRIPT's more advanced text handling features, including string-slicing with the **getinterval** operator, advanced print positioning with **widthshow** and performing an operation on every character in a string with **forall**.

This program operates in a similar way to the previous one, but with added sophistication. When a line can take no more words without exceeding the given line length, the text is padded out evenly to exactly fill the given line length. The text aligns neatly at both the left and right margins. This is called **justified** text.

In this program, unlike the last, the current line is stored as a whole before being printed out, so that the padding operation can be carried out by the procedure **pad** before the line is printed.

```
% Justified text

/justify
{
  /points exch def          % get point size from stack
  /margin exch def          % get left margin from stack
  /llength exch def         % get line length from stack
  /ypos exch def            % get initial y position from stack
  /ycur ypos def            % define current y position
  /line 200 string def      % blank string for this line
  /lcount 0 def             % character count in line
  /wcount 0 def             % character count in word
  /spaces -1 def            % number of spaces in line
  /word 20 string def       % blank word

  /pad
  {
    /lcount lcount 1 sub def
    line 0 lcount            % delete last space
    getinterval
    /line exch def           % and get line again
    llength                  % get max line length
    line 0 lcount getinterval
    stringwidth pop          % get width of current line
    /spaces spaces 1 sub def
    sub spaces div           % subtract and div by spaces
    0 32 line widthshow      % show with extra width
  } def

  /addword
  {
    line lcount word 0 wcount
    getinterval putinterval % add word onto line string
    wcount lcount add        % update line length
    /lcount exch def
    /wcount 0 def            % reset word length
    /word 20 string def      % blank word variable
  } def

  /leading                  % set leading at 2 points
  points 2 add              %    greater than point size
  def

  /newline                  % proc for line break
```

```
{                         % proc start
  /ycur                   % drop y position by leading
  ycur leading sub
  def
  margin ycur             % move down and back to margin
  moveto
  ycur 100 lt             % ypos <100 pts to page end?
  {
    /ycur ypos def        % yes, reset current position
    showpage              %     print current page
    margin ycur moveto    %     and move to page head
  } if
  /spaces 0 def
  /line 200 string def    % empty current line
  /lcount 0 def           % line length = 0
  addword
} def                     % end of newline proc

/Times-Roman findfont     % set font for text
points scalefont setfont

( ) stringwidth pop       % get width of a space
/gap exch def

margin ypos moveto        % move to start point

{
  /char exch def          % get character
  word wcount             % put char on end of word
  char put
  /wcount wcount 1 add def% increment word counter
  char 32 eq              % is it a space?
  {                       % if so, then....
    /spaces               % incr. spaces in line
    spaces 1 add
    def
    line 0 lcount
    getinterval           % get current line text

    stringwidth pop       % get current line length
    word 0 wcount
    getinterval           % get word width

    stringwidth pop       % get word length
```

```
   add                        % add them
   gap sub                    % less the last space
   llength gt                 % longer than max line length?
   {                          % if so, then...
     pad                      % pad out line and print it
     newline                  % carriage return line feed
   }
   {addword} ifelse           % less than max length, add word
  } if                        % if not a space, carry on
 } forall                     %    and do the rest
 addword line show
} def


(As I walked through the wilderness of this world, \
I lighted on a certain place, where was a den; \
and I laid me down in that place to sleep: and as I \
slept I dreamed a dream. I dreamed, and behold I saw \
a man clothed with rags, standing in a certain place, with \
his face from his own house, a book in his hand, and a \
great burden upon his back. I looked, and saw him open the \
book, and read therein; and as he read, he wept and \
trembled: and not being able longer to contain, he brake \
out with a lamentable cry; saying, 'What shall I do?' )


% NOTE: THE TEXT MUST END WITH A SPACE


740                          % y start position
450                          % line length
75                           % left margin
32                           % point size


justify
newline                      % blank line
newline
/Times-Italic findfont       % set font for credit
points 0.75 mul scalefont
setfont
(The Pilgrim's Progress, John Bunyan) show


showpage
```

The program starts by assigning variables for the point size, left margin, line length, and start position. Next come the sub-procedures:

pad removes the last character from the line (a space) before finding the distance in points by which it falls short of the given line length. This distance is divided by the number of spaces. The relevant number of points is then added to each occurrence of space in the line by using **widthshow**.

addword places the contents of the **word** string on the end of the current **line** string. The variable for the current line length is updated to include the new word; the variable for the word length is zeroed and the **word** string redefined as blank.

newline, as in the previous program, performs an intelligent carriage return/line feed. It checks that the new y position is not within 50 points of the page end. If it is, the current page is printed, the y position reset to the top of the page and the program continues. If not, the line variables are reset and the word added to the now blank line.

Times is selected at the given point size. A space is measured for width - this is used when checking to see if a word will overstep the line length. The main routine then takes each character in the given text string, adding it first to the word, then, at each occurrence of a space, checking line lengths. The word is either added to the line or placed on a new line after the old line is padded and printed.

At the end of the loop, the remaining part line is printed, followed by a blank line and the credit.

CIRCULAR TEXT

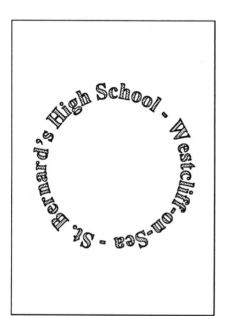

This program demonstrates the positioning of text in other than the usual portrait or landscape orientations by using the **rotate** operator to rotate the coordinate system of user space.

The program prints a given text string clockwise around the circumference of an undrawn circle and centered around the top of the circle. The procedure as it appears here prints the text in outline (see the program under the heading Simple Text at the start of this chapter), although this may be changed to solid text by removing the **oshow** procedure and substituting the **show** operator.

No range checking is carried out on the values given for the point size and the circle, so if your text surrounds more than one circumference of the circle at the stated point size, then the text will simply overlap itself.

```
% Circle Text

/circletext
{
  /points exch def          % get point size from stack
  /radius exch def          % get circle radius from stack
  /text exch def            % get text string from stack
  /char 0 def               % for current ASCII value
  /str 1 string def         % for current char string
  /pi 3.14159 def           % value of pi
  /circum                   % calculate circumference
  radius 2 mul pi mul
  def

  /oshow
  {
    true charpath gsave       % create outline path & save
    0.8 setgray fill grestore % fill path with gray; restore
    stroke
  } def


  /Times-Bold findfont      % select Times
  points scalefont setfont  %   at given point size

  300 420 translate         % move origin to center of A4 page
  text stringwidth pop      % get total width of text
  2 div                     % halve it
  circum div 360 mul        % get angle that the text surrounds
  rotate                    % rotate back for start point

  text                      % stack the given text
  {                         % main procedure
    /char exch def          % get a character
    0 radius moveto         % move to edge of circle
    str 0 char put          % put character in string
    str stringwidth pop     % get its width
    circum div 360 mul      % find the angle it surrounds
    /charot exch def        % define character rotation
    gsave                   % save graphics state
    0 radius translate      % origin to edge of circle
    charot 2 div neg rotate % rot. 1/2 angle for char
    str oshow               % so char sits tangentially
    grestore                %   then show it and restore
```

```
     charot                % rot. value for current char
     neg rotate            % go clockwise
   } forall                % proc end
 } def

 ( - St. Bernard's High School - Westcliff-on-Sea)
 200                       % radius
 63                        % point size

 circletext
 showpage
```

The program starts by assigning variables for the point size, circle radius and text. Variables are also assigned for the ASCII value of the current character, its string representation, an approximation to Pi and the circumference of the circle.

The **oshow** procedure prints text in outline only, this is seen in the first program in this chapter, under the heading Simple Text. Note, however, that small point sizes may appear rather messy using this method. To use solid characters, remove the **oshow** procedure and replace the single occurrence of **oshow** in the main program with the **show** operator.

Times is selected and scaled to the given point size. The origin is moved to the center of the A4 page, this is also the center of the base circle around which the text falls. The full width of the given string is then calculated. This is used to center the text around the vertical, rather than starting at the top of the circle and rolling around to some unspecified end.

The main procedure takes each character of the string in turn, moves to the edge of the circle and puts the character into a one element string. The width of this string is found and an angle calculated from the amount of the circle's circumference that the current character will cover. The graphics state is then saved.

The origin is moved to the start point of the current character. This allows us to rotate the character so that it sits tangentially to the circle. In fact, the characters do cross the circle slightly as the base of the character forms a chord to the circle. The character is shown and the previous graphics state restored. The graphics state is then rotated by the width of the character at the edge of the circle, ready for the next character.

When the whole string has been wrapped around the circle, the page is printed out.

CHARACTER TRANSFORMATIONS

Normal
bɘꙅ𝗋ɘvɘЯ
Backslant
Uphill
Reflection

As a final example of POSTSCRIPT's text handling abilities, this program demonstrates the effects of a number of different matrix transformations on the Helvetica font. All of these examples use the **makefont** operator to transform the usual character definitions with a given matrix. This allows us to italicise, invert, rotate, reflect and otherwise rearrange any of the fonts available on the output device.

To make full use of the POSTSCRIPT operators which use matrices in this way, a basic knowledge of their mathematics is useful, but not essential. Some interesting effects can be achieved very simply.

The program starts by showing the word Normal in the basic Helvetica font at 80 points. Helvetica is selected and scaled in the usual way with the **findfont, scalefont** and **setfont** operators. The rest of the examples use the **makefont** operator to transform the characters by a given matrix.

Using **makefont** in this way allows us to scale a font in the x direction for example, like we did in the first program in this chapter, but without scaling the whole x axis. This means that other fonts used and any graphics will retain their true proportions. It also allows us to distort the characters in other ways, again without affecting the current graphics state.

```
% Transformed Text

/Helvetica findfont          % normal text first
80 scalefont setfont
100 680 moveto
(Normal) show

/reverse
{
  /Helvetica findfont
  [-80 0 0 80 0 0] makefont% reverse characters
  setfont
  dup
  stringwidth pop            % find start x position
  neg 0 rmoveto show
} def

/backslant
{
  /Helvetica findfont
  [80 0 -35 80 0 0] makefont % reverse italicise characters
  setfont show
} def

/uphill
{
  /Helvetica findfont
  [80 50 0 80 0 0] makefont% skew characters
  setfont show
} def

/reflect
{
  /Helvetica findfont
  [80 0 0 -80 0 80] makefont % reflect characters
  setfont show
} def
```

```
100 580 moveto
(Reversed) reverse
100 480 moveto
(Backslant) backslant
100 260 moveto
(Uphill) uphill
100 160 moveto
(Reflection) reflect
showpage
```

The program creates four procedures, **reversed, backslant, uphill** and **reflect**: their effects on the text given them are obvious from the names. Each takes the basic Helvetica font and applies a matrix transformation to the characters of that font. Any of these procedures could be incorporated into your own programs using the same or another font.

3. USING GRAPHICS

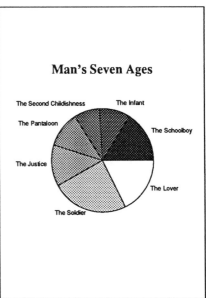

This chapter includes a number of graphics programs which can be used as they appear here, or may be adapted to produce the type of output you require.

For further details of any of the operators used, refer to chapter 5 where all of the POSTSCRIPT operators and their syntax are described. Some of the programs can be combined with others to produce a different output. For example, one of the bar charts could be printed with a frame around the page by the inclusion of the frame program.

The programs included in this chapter have been written with an A4 laser printer in mind as the target device. They will, however, work with most POSTSCRIPT devices. If you intend to produce output on any other device, take care to follow any device-dependent procedures required by that device.

PLAIN PAGE FRAME

This program produces a plain line frame around an A4 page approximately 10mm from the edge of the sheet. The program demonstrates the use of basic line drawing using **moveto, rlineto** and **stroke.**

Some POSTSCRIPT devices have a non-printing margin around the edge of a page. This program should allow the whole frame to be seen on most laser printers.

The examples above show the edge of the paper (outer line) and the frame drawn by the program (inner line). The example on the left is from the program as given here. In the example on the right, the line width setting has been set to 4 points by changing the figure in the first line of the **plainframe** procedure.

```
% A4 Page Plain Frame

/plainframe
{
```

```
1.5 setlinewidth       % set the frame line width
newpath                % start the path
30 30 moveto           % move to the bottom left corner
540 0 rlineto          % draw to the bottom right corner
0 780 rlineto          % draw to the top right corner
-540 0 rlineto         % draw to the top left corner
closepath              % close frame with neat mitre
stroke                 % stroke onto page
} def

plainframe
showpage
```

The line width used is 1.5 points. This value may be increased or decreased for a thicker or thinner frame line. A value of 0 produces a line one pixel wide on the output device. Note that on high resolution devices, such fine lines may be difficult to see!

The program starts a new path for the frame, moves to the lower left corner of the frame and draws the four lines. The box is finished with the **closepath** operator and then rendered onto the page with the **stroke** operator.

The page, with its frame, is then printed out.

FADED PAGE FRAME

This program produces a line frame around an A4 page which fades out towards the edge of the page, stopping approximately 10mm from the edge of the sheet. The program demonstrates the use of the **setgray** operator to produce output in various shades of gray; the use of the **gsave** and **grestore** operators to save and restore the graphics state; the **scale** operator to reduce the scale of the final printed image and the **for** operator to create a looping structure.

The example above shows the edge of the paper (outer line) and the frame drawn by the program on the inside.

```
% A4 Page Fade In Frame

/fadeframe
{
  gsave                         % save graphics state
  300 420 translate             % move origin to page centre
```

```
1.5 setlinewidth        % width of overlapping lines
   1 -0.05 0            % settings for setgray
   {
     newpath            % new path for each box
     setgray            % takes setting from stack
     -270 -390 moveto   % move to bottom left of frame
     540 0 rlineto      % draw bottom edge
     0 780 rlineto      %    right edge
     -540 0 rlineto     %    top edge
     closepath          % and left with closepath
     stroke             % stroke box onto page
     0.998 dup scale    % scale down for next one in
   } for                %    and repeat
   grestore             % restore gray level + origin
} def

fadeframe
showpage                % print page
```

This program starts by saving the whole of the current graphics state. This means that when that state is restored later, the origin moves back to its previous position (the bottom left of the page), the gray level is reset to black and the scale of the final image (1:1) is reset.

The origin is moved to the centre of the page to allow each successive box to be centred on the previous ones. A line width of 1.5 points allows each successive gray line to just overlap the previous one. A greater value would provide exactly the same faded area but with a heavier black line on the inside as this line is not overlapped by any other.

The next part of the program forms a looping structure. The three numbers represent the start, increment and end of a series of numbers which are given in turn to the following procedure. The procedure sets the gray level for each box, draws the box and shrinks the overall scale of the image down by a small amount. Successive boxes then lie inside and overlap slightly the previous ones. The last, inner box is black.

The program ends by restoring the graphics state.

To change the direction of the fade, so that the outer box is black fading to white inside, replace the program line shown bold above with the following:

```
    0  0.05 1              % gray settings for fade in
```

For a broader faded area, change the middle of these three numbers to a smaller number; halving the middle number doubles the width of the frame.

POLYGON

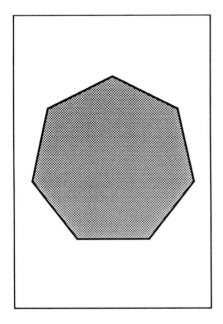

This program will draw an accurate regular polygon with any number of sides from three upwards. (2 sides produces a straight line; 1 side produces no output.) The program builds on the experience gained in the previous programs, using line drawing, filling with gray and using looping structures and introduces the ability to rotate user space with the **rotate** operator.

The main procedure, **polygon** assumes the presence of three objects on the stack; the diameter of the smallest circle which would enclose the required polygon, the number of sides and the level of gray with which the finished polygon will be filled.

```
% Polygon

/polygon
{
 gsave
  /graylev exch def          % get gray level for fill
```

```
/sides exch def          % get number of sides
/diameter exch def       % get diam of bounding circle
/radius diameter 2 div def % calc radius of circle
/angle 360 sides div def % calc step angle

300 420 translate        % origin to page centre

0 sin radius mul
0 cos radius mul moveto  % get start point

0 angle 360              % 0 to 360 in steps of angle
{
  dup                    % duplicate angle for x & y
  sin radius mul exch    % x position of next corner
  cos radius mul         % y position of next corner
  lineto                 % draw side
} for
closepath                % neat mitre on rejoin

gsave                    % save outline
graylev setgray fill     % fill outline
grestore                 % restore outline
stroke                   % stroke onto page
grestore
} def

500 7 0.8 polygon
showpage
```

The procedure **polygon** starts by saving the graphics state for later restoration, because the origin and gray level are changed during the procedure's operation. Next the three values are taken off the stack and assigned to the variables **graylev**, **sides** and **diameter**. The radius of the bounding circle is then calculated and the step angle for each side of the polygon.

The origin is moved to the centre of the A4 page, which will coincide with the centre of the polygon. The main loop draws each side of the polygon in turn, stepping around the circle as many times as necessary to complete the shape, drawing one side of the polygon with each step.

The graphics state is re-saved, the gray level set and the polygon filled. The graphics state is then restored and stroked with the outline of the polygon. Finally the original graphics state is restored.

STACKED BAR CHART

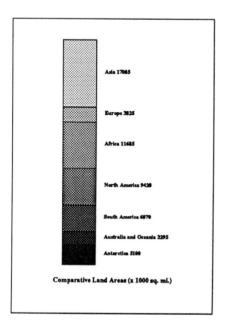

This program produces a single stack bar chart, each section being filled to a different gray shade. Each section has a label, positioned to the right and half way up the height of the section. The chart has a title at the bottom of the page.

The program demonstrates the conversion of numbers into printable text, the use of the **counttomark** operator to count the number of parameters given to the main procedure and **copy** to copy that number of items on the stack.

```
% Stacked Bar

/stackbar
{
  /title exch def        % get graph title
  counttomark 2 idiv     % count items to show in chart
  /number exch def       % assign to number
  /width 100 def         % width of bar
```

```
/xpos
200 width 2 div sub
def                     % get x position of left side
/vpos 140 def           % set baseline
/total 0 def            % for total of numerics
/grayinc                % get gray increment
1 number div
def
/currgray
grayinc 2 div
def                     % for current gray shade

/item
{
  newpath 0 setgray     % set black for outline
  xpos width add 25 add vpos
  moveto                % go to right of current item
  exch                  % number over string
  /value exch def       % get current value
  0 value
  factor mul 2 div rmoveto% move up half height of item
  show
  /svalue 10 string def % for str. val of current item
  value svalue cvs      % copy current value to string
  ( ) show show         % space & cur. val as string
  xpos vpos moveto      % to bottom left of cur. item
  width 0 rlineto       % draw box...
  0 value factor mul rlineto
  width neg 0 rlineto
  closepath
  gsave                 % save outline
  currgray setgray      % set gray shade
  fill grestore         % fill bar & restore key-line
  stroke
  /currgray             % increment gray level for
  currgray grayinc      %   next bar
  add
  def
  /vpos
  vpos value factor
  mul add
  def                   % update vertical position
}
def
```

```
/Times-Bold
findfont 24 scalefont
setfont                      % set font for title

title dup stringwidth pop% get width of title
2 div 300 exch sub 90 moveto    % pos'n for start of title
show                         % show title

/Times-Bold
findfont 16 scalefont
setfont                      % font for labels

number 2 mul 1 add copy   % duplicate contents
number                    % ready to add them up
{
  pop total add
  /total exch def
} repeat                  % get total of values

640 total div             % get multip. factor for chart
/factor exch def
pop                       % remove top mark

number {item} repeat      % draw chart
pop                       % remove mark
stroke
} def

mark                      % start of values on stack
17085   (Asia)
3825    (Europe)
11685   (Africa)
9420    (North America)
6870    (South America)
3295    (Australia and Oceania)
5100    (Antarctica)
(Comparative Land Areas \(x 1000 sq. mi.\))

stackbar
showpage
```

The program starts by taking the chart title off the stack. Then a number of variables are defined: chart width, x position of the left side of the chart, baseline and total of all the numeric values. The last of these is used when calculating the multiplication factor for the height of the sections.

The procedure **item**, defined next, draws the sections and fills them and positions and prints the labels. First the gray level is set to black for the outline of the section. The current point is then positioned for the text label. This is followed by a space and the text representation of the numeric value of the section. Another variable is used for this string - in this case, defined within the main procedure. This is to ensure that it is cleared before being used for each section.

The section itself is then drawn and the graphics state saved, the section filled and the outline restored. Lastly, the vertical position is updated to the bottom of the next section, ready for the next value pair.

Times-Roman at 24 points is selected as the font for the chart title. The title is centred at the bottom of the page. The font is then selected for the section labels. Again the font is Times, but at a smaller point size.

The contents of the stack down to the **mark** is then duplicated. This gives us one set of data which can be used to find the total of all the numeric values and another set for drawing the actual chart. So next, the total of the numerics is found, this giving us a multiplication factor when divided into the maximum chart height of 640 points.

The top mark is removed and each value pair dealt with by the procedure **item**. When the final **mark** is removed from the stack, the page is printed.

BAR CHART

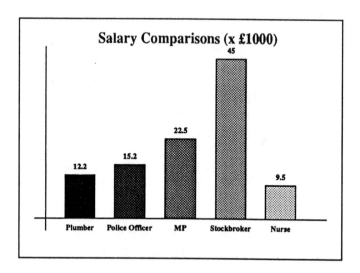

This program produces a side-by-side bar chart. Each bar has a label beneath and its numeric value printed above. Note that due to the order in which the items are placed on the stack, the last item in the list of chart items is the first to be drawn and appears at the left of the chart.

```
% Bar chart

/barchart
{
  /title exch def           % get graph title
  counttomark 2 idiv        % get number of value pairs
  /number exch def
  /grayinc 1 number div def % for gray shade increment
  /currgray grayinc 2 div def    % for current gray shade
  /high 0 def               % for highest value
  /value 0 def              % for current value

  /bar                      % draw bar; fill; top label
  {
    /value exch def         % get current value from stack
    newpath
    0 setgray               % black line for edge
```

```
width 0.4 mul 0 moveto    % move to left edge of bar
width 0.6 mul 0 rlineto   % draw base
0 value factor mul rlineto     % draw right edge
width 0.6 mul neg
0 rlineto                 % draw top
closepath                 % draw left edge

gsave                     % save everything
currgray setgray          % set gray shade
fill grestore             % fill bar; restore key-line
stroke closepath
/currgray                 % increment gray level for
currgray grayinc add      %   next bar
def

/svalue 20 string def     % for string version of values
value svalue cvs          % make string from value
dup stringwidth pop       % get width of value string
width 0.7 mul exch
2 div sub                 % get start point of string
value factor
mul 15 add moveto         % go there
show                      %   and show label
} def

/label                    % print label below bar
{
  dup stringwidth pop     % get width of label
  width 0.7 mul exch
  2 div sub               % get start point of label
  -30 moveto              % go there
  show                    %   and show label
} def

number 2 mul 1 add copy   % duplicate values and mark
number                    %   to find highest value
{
  pop dup                 % discard label & copy cur val
  high gt                 % compare cur. val with high
  {/high exch def}        % current  high
  {pop}                   % high  current
  ifelse                  % checking
} repeat
pop                       % remove top mark
```

```
400 high div              % get mult. factor for values
/factor exch def          % and assign to factor

650 number div            % width of bar & space
/width exch def           % and assign to width

90 rotate                 % go landscape
70 -500 translate         % move graph origin
1.5 setlinewidth          % line width for axes
0 -30 moveto 0 460 rlineto % draw y axis
-30 0 moveto 760 0 rlineto % draw x axis
stroke                    %    and stroke them

/Times-Bold findfont      % font for title
36 scalefont setfont
title
dup stringwidth pop       % get width of title
2 div 370 exch sub
440 moveto                % get start of title
show                      %    and show it

/Times-Bold findfont      % label font
20 scalefont setfont
2 setlinewidth            % linewidth for bars

number                    % main proc this many times
{
  label                   % show centred label
  bar                     % draw bar
  width 0 translate       % move across for next
} repeat
pop                       % discard mark
grestore
} def

mark
9.5     (Nurse)
45      (Stockbroker)
22.5    (MP)
15.2    (Police Officer)
12.2    (Plumber)
(Salary Comparisons \(x \2431000\))
```

```
barchart
showpage
```

The program starts, like the single stack chart, by taking the chart title off the stack. In this example, we want to include a pound sign (£), and as this falls outside the basic character set of most laser printers, we have to insert the character manually. This is done by including a backslash followed by the octal code (243) for the pound character.

A number of variables are now identified; the greatest value in the chart, the current value and the number of value pairs. These are followed by two procedures, **bar** and **label**. **bar** draws the bar, shades it with a gray level, increments the gray level for the next bar, and prints the text representation of the current value at the top of the bar. **label** centres and prints the text label beneath the current bar.

Next the contents of the stack down to and including the **mark** are duplicated in preparation for finding the highest numeric value. This is done by keeping a high value (**high**) and comparing this with each numeric value (**value**) in turn. If a value is greater than the high, the value becomes the new high. The high enables us to calculate the multiplication factor for the bar height. The chart will then neatly fit within an A4 page. Also, the width of bar is calculated according to the number of bars to be drawn.

Note that 10 to 14 bars may be drawn if their labels are kept short. If long labels are used, they may overlap each other between the bars.

The page is rotated through 90 degrees to landscape format and the axes drawn. Times at 36 points is selected for the graph title and the title centred at the top of the graph. Times at 20 point is used for the text labels and the numerics at the top of each bar. The line width is set for the border of each bar.

Finally, to draw the bars and position the labels, the last section of the program executes the procedures **label** and **bar** as many times as there are value pairs, moving across each time by the appropriate distance. Finally the last **mark** is removed from the stack.

PIE CHART

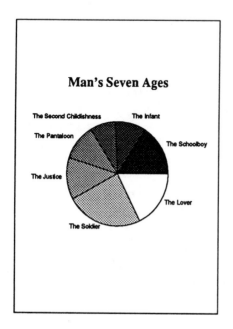

The program adds up the supplied numeric values and allots a percentage of the circle to each value pair. Each slice is edged with a key-line and shaded gray. Successive slices are shaded in turn from near-black to white. The labels are centred at the edge of the slice. If your chart has more than about 25 values, the slice labels may overlap. This problem can be avoided by using a smaller point size for the labels.

```
% Pie Chart

/piechart
{
  gsave
  /title exch def           % get chart title
  counttomark 2 idiv        % count number of value pairs
  /number exch def
  /value 0 def              % for current value
```

```
/total 0 def              % total of values
/rothalf 0 def            % half rot'n for current slice
/totrot 0 def             % total rotation so far
/grayinc                  % get gray increment
1 number div
def
/currgray grayinc def     % for cur. gray shade

/slice
{
  0 0 moveto              % move to origin
  0 0 150 0 rot arc
  0 0 lineto              % draw arc & back to origin
  gsave
  currgray setgray        % set gray shade
  fill grestore           % fill bar; restore key-line
  stroke
  /currgray               % increment gray level for
  currgray grayinc        %    next slice
  add
  def
} def

/dolabel
{
  gsave                   % save current state
  165 0 translate         % origin outside slice
  0 0 moveto              % move to origin
  totrot neg rotate       % rotate back so label level
  totrot 90 gt            % is current label...
  totrot 270 lt           %    to left of chart? and
  {                       % if so, then...
    label                 % get width of label
    stringwidth
    pop                   % discard y height
    neg 0 rmoveto         % move left by width of label
  } if
  label show              % print label
  grestore                % restore previous state
} def

300 400 translate         % move origin
1 setlinewidth            % line width for key-line
```

```
/Times-Bold findfont         % get title font
28 scalefont setfont         % scale to 20 pt
title stringwidth pop        % get title width
2 div neg 250 moveto         % centre title
title show                   % print title

/Helvetica findfont          % get title font
14 scalefont setfont         % scale to 12 pt

number 2 mul 1 add copy      % copy stack contents

number                       % number of value pairs
{                            % repeat start
  pop                        % discard label
  /total                     % add next value to total
  exch total add
  def
} repeat

pop                          % remove top mark
/factor
360 total div def            % get multiplication factor

number                       % number of sectors
{                            % start repeat
  /label exch def
  label stringwidth pop      % get width of label
  /labelwid exch def         % and assign to labelwid
  /value exch def            % get current value
  value factor mul           % multiply by factor
  /rot exch def              % call it rotation
  /rothalf
  rot 2 div def              % get half rotation

  slice                      % draw slice

  /totrot
  totrot rothalf add         % update rotation so far
  def
  rothalf rotate             % rotate to half current value
  dolabel                    % position and print label
  rothalf rotate             % rotate other half of current
  /totrot                    %    value and update total
  totrot rothalf add         %    rotation so far
```

```
   def
 } repeat
 pop                          % remove last mark
 grestore
} def

mark
11      (The Lover)
15      (The Soldier)
8       (The Justice)
7       (The Pantaloon)
5       (The Second Childishness)
6       (The Infant)
10      (The Schoolboy)
(The Seven Ages of Man)

piechart
showpage
```

The program begins by saving the graphics state (the program moves the origin to the centre of the page) and taking the chart title off the stack. Next the number of value pairs is found and a range of variables assigned: the number of value pairs, numeric total, half the angle of the current slice, total rotation so far, the increment for the gray shading of each slice and the current gray level. The procedures which follow operate as follows:

slice sets the current point to the origin (page centre), draws the slice, saves the graphics state to preserve the key-line, fills the slice with the current gray setting, restores the graphics state and strokes the completed slice.

dolabel does just that; it saves the current graphics state, moves the origin out to the edge of the current slice and rotates the page round so that the label, when printed, will be level. If the centre of the current slice is to the left of the centre of the pie, the label is positioned so that it does not cross the pie. The label is printed and the graphics state restored, moving the origin back to the centre of the pie.

The origin is placed at the centre of the page and the line width for the slice key-lines is set. Helvetica is selected and scaled for the chart title, and this is printed. Again Helvetica is selected for the slice labels, but at a smaller point size.

The contents of the stack down to and including the **mark** are copied. The first set of data is then used to calculate the total of the numeric values and, from that, the multiplication factor which gives the angle of slice from each numeric value. The top **mark** is removed from the stack and discarded.

The main part of the program operates on each value pair in turn, positioning the label to correspond to the centre of the slice, calling the procedures **slice** and **dolabel** and updating the variable for total rotation so far. Finally, the **mark** is removed from the stack.

USING CURVETO

The following examples and program simply give an indication of the power of the POSTSCRIPT operator **curveto**. The pattern produced by the program can be repeated, scaled or drawn in shades of gray for use, for example, as a page border. But first, to describe how **curveto** operates.

The **curveto** operator takes three pairs of points in the coordinate system as its operands. The fourth, unstated, operand is the current point. The four points enclose an external quadrilateral which completely encloses the curve produced by the operator. Point 1 is the current point and points 2 to 4 are given as operands to **curveto**. The resulting line starts at point 1, tangential to a straight line between points 1 and 2. It veers towards point 3 and finally connects with point 4, tangential to a straight line between points 3 and 4.

Here are two examples. The points are labelled and the curves take the course described above. The straight lines and the circles at the junctions are for information only - they are not produced by **curveto**.

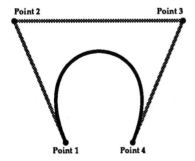
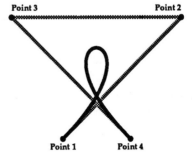

CURVETO PATTERN

This program produces a double looped curve which can be repeated any number of times to produce, for example, an ornate page border. Here, the pattern is repeated just three times to give an idea of how the pattern might look. Each iteration of the main procedure produces a loop to each side of the longditudinal centre line.

```
% Curveto Pattern

/ctpattern
{
  90 rotate                % landscape orientation
  120 -300 translate       % x axis to centre of page
  9 setlinewidth           % thick line
  1 setlinecap             % round line caps

  3                        % 3 iterations of procedure
  {
```

```
0 0 moveto              % current point
400 200                 % point 1
-300 200                % point 2
100 0                   % point 3
curveto                 % draw curve

100 0 translate         % move across for other half

0 0 moveto              % current point
400 -200                % point 1
-300 -200               % point 2
100 0                   % point 3
curveto                 % draw curve

100 0 translate         % across for next iteration
} repeat
stroke
} def

ctpattern
showpage
```

The program first rotates the axis around by 90 degrees and sets the origin at the centre line of the page. The line width is set to 9 and rounded line-caps specified. Each iteration of the main procedure moves the origin along the length of the page to a new start point. About 3 repetitions of the pattern will fit on the A4 page as the program stands. This number may be increased by scaling the x axis down.

The main procedure sets the current point at the origin and specifies the x and y coordinates of the three points for the first curve. These are dealt with by the first **curveto**. The origin is then moved forward to the starting point for the other half of the pattern. Again the current point is moved to the origin and three points specified. The second **curveto** produces a mirror image of the first half of the pattern, but moved along by 100 points.

The origin is moved along once more and the procedure ends. Finally, the pattern is stroked and printed out.

Try changing the distance by which the origin is moved each time. This will give a multiple pattern effect, but you may need to increase the number of iterations to produce an acceptable pattern.

BITMAPPED GRAPHICS

POSTSCRIPT has two operators which enable raw hexadecimal data to be built up into bit-mapped images; **imagemask** and **image**. The first of these takes one byte of hexadecimal data and produces from it eight image pixels, one bit per pixel. The second operator takes one byte of hexadecimal data and applies either 1, 2, 4 or 8 bits to each image pixel, giving 2, 4, 16 or 256 gray levels per pixel.

Mask Graphics

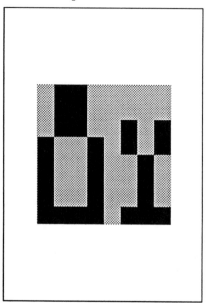

This program uses the **imagemask** operator to render a binary bit map image onto the page. Each bit in the supplied data provides one pixel of the image - a 1 makes a black pixel and a 0 does nothing. Note that zeros do not render a white pixel, blotting out any previous material underneath; they simply do not have any effect other than to provide blank space between the 1's in the data.

In the program a gray square is first drawn and filled, providing a visible background over which the binary image is rendered. For further details of the **imagemask** operator, see chapter 5.

```
% Mask Graphics

/mgraphic
{
  gsave
  100 220 translate           % move origin up & right

  0 0 moveto                  % bottom left corner of image
  400 0 rlineto               % draw a box and shade in
  0 400 rlineto               %    to act as a background
  -400 0 rlineto              %    to the binary bitmapped
  0 0 lineto                  %    image
  0.8 setgray fill

  400 400 scale               % expand image to req. size

  0 setgray                   % ON bits are black
  0 0 moveto                  % bottom left corner of image

  8                           % width in bits
  8                           % height in bits
  true                        % invert (true=ON bits black)
  [8 0 0 -8 0 8]              % transform to image coords

  {
    60606595
    929292F7
  }                           % end bit data
  imagemask
  grestore
} def

mgraphic
showpage
```

The program starts by saving the graphics state and moving the origin up and to the right. The origin sits at the lower left hand corner of the square image. A box is drawn 400 points square and filled with gray. The image, which initially renders into a one point square, is then scaled up to fit the gray square.

The gray level is reset to black and the parameters for **imagemask** placed on the stack. These are the coordinates of the bottom left corner of the image, the width and height of the image in bits and the inversion status. The last of these is a boolean;

true renders 1's as black pixels and 0's as transparent pixels, false renders 0's black and 1's as transparent pixels.

Note that no comments should be included on the lines containing the hex data as these will cause an error.

When the image is complete, the graphics state is resored to reset the origin to the bottom left of the page.

Gray Scale Bit Graphics

The second bit image operator, **image**, produces images where each pixel is rendered with one of a number of shades of gray. Images may be produced with 2, 4, 16 or 256 levels of gray per pixel, with a resulting increase in the amount of data needed for a given size of image as the number of gray shades increases.

Producing gray-scale images with the **image** operator leads to higher quality images, but takes rather longer due to the larger amounts of data being handled by POSTSCRIPT. Obviously, producing an image at 256 gray levels per pixel will take much longer than one with just two possible levels per pixel (black and white) as 8 times as much data must be processed to produce the image.

This program produces an image using 8 bits per pixel, two hex digits (one byte) are required for each pixel of the image.

```
% Grey Scale Graphics

/ggraphic
{
  gsave
  100 220 translate        % origin to bot. left of image
  0 0 moveto               % move to origin
  /str 4 string def        % string for data
  400 400 scale            % size of image

  4 4                      % width and height in pixels
  8                        % bits per pixel
  [4 0 0 -4 0 4]           % mapping into device space

  {
    currentfile str
    readhexstring pop
  }                        % data reading procedure
  image

  F0DFBF9F
  DFBF9F7F
  BF9F7F54
  9F7F5432
  grestore                 % restore scale and origin
} def

ggraphic
showpage
```

The program begins by saving the graphics state and moving the origin up and to the right. The origin will be at the lower left hand corner of the image. A blank string is created to contain the data to be read from the input file, and the image scaled to a suitable size.

The width and height of the image (in pixels) are followed by the number of bits per pixel. This determines the number of possible levels of gray per pixel. If you use, for example, 4 bits per pixel, the information for the first pixel is taken from the high nibble of the first hex byte of data; the information for the second pixel is taken from the low nibble of the same byte. If your image is an odd number of pixels wide, then the last byte must be packed with four dummy bits to make up a full byte. These bits are discarded when the last pixel has been rendered.

The transformation matrix then follows. Next is the procedure which reads the data from the input file. The data is again in hexadecimal format. When the correct amount of data has been read, the image is complete and the graphics state is restored.

4. BUILDING A NEW FONT

BUYING FONTS

Some POSTSCRIPT printers have a very limited number of typefaces, or fonts, as standard. This number can be increased by buying new fonts, either on some magnetic media which is fitted to the printer, or on disk which are downloaded from a computer. Alternatively, you can design and build your own new font. This chapter shows how a new font can be built from scratch fairly simply, and then used to create a variety of effects.

When you buy a new font for, for example, a POSTSCRIPT laser printer, the font is supplied on disk. The description of the font is then downloaded to the printer each time it is used. This can be quite time consuming, and, if a number of fonts are to be added, quite expensive.

BUILDING FONTS

There are two ways of building a new typeface using POSTSCRIPT; the first is to create a new font from scratch using the POSTSCRIPT operators **definefont**, **makefont** and so on. A full example of this type of operation is beyond the scope of this book. The second, and rather simpler option, is to build a limited new font by using a short procedure to draw each character in the alphabet. The procedure which draws the letter a is called **a**, the procedure for b is called **b** and so on through the alphabet.

On the previous page is an example of the sort of output which can be achieved from a user-defined font.

Many of the same effects can be used with a user-defined font as with the built-in POSTSCRIPT fonts; text can be printed in any shade from white to black, expanded or contracted in the x or y direction, in a variety of weights and in varying sizes. Fonts built in this way can be printed at any size with no loss of smoothness on curves or oblique strokes, because the full power of POSTSCRIPT is used when drawing each individual character.

A NEW FONT

```
malcolm is crying
joan is nice
sarah can sing
geoff rides a bicycle
fiona is on holiday
barry is working
rory is old
shula is lovely
sukie is invisible
```

This font, called LowerSchool, is based on very simple geometry; all curves (except the s) are based on a single circle, most characters have the same width and only lower case letters are used. This font could usefully be used for signs and notices for young children.

To build the characters, rather than draw each one from scratch, a number of 'components' have been used. Two letters use a short stroke at the right of the character; the first of these is the letter a, so a procedure is written, called **abar**. Other common features are the 'a circle' (**acirc**) and stroke of the b (**bbar**) curve of the h (**hcurv**).

To move the current point (lower left corner of the character space) across when the letter has been drawn, a number of standard character widths are defined. Each of these has its own procedure. This makes it a simple matter to update the position of the current point ready for the next character.

The procedures which draw the letters themselves are named using the appropriate letters, **a** for the letter a, **b** for the letter b and so on. These are executed by a shell procedure, **showit,** which takes a text string and breaks it down into its component characters. Each of these in turn is then converted into an executable object of the same name and placed on the execution stack. Procedures are also defined to carry out carriage return/line feed (**newline**) and form feed (**newpage**) operations.

For economy of space, the program here has few comments, but there are notes at the end which explain its use.

```
% new typeface

/LowerSchool
{
  /margin exch def          /points exch def
  /weight exch def          /ytop exch def
  /xpos margin def          /ypos ytop def
  /ppt66 points 0.666 mul def
  /ppt33 points 0.333 mul def
  /pts points def           /rad ppt33 def
  /ppt72 points 0.72 mul def /ppt8 points 0.8 mul def
  /str 1 string def         /ppt166 points 0.166 mul def

  /newpage {/ypos ytop def points 50 div
  eight mul setlinewidth
  1 setlinecap 1 setlinejoin} def

  /newline {/xpos margin def /ypos ypos points 1.5 mul
  sub def ypos 100 lt { showpage newpage} if} def
  /k75 {/xpos xpos pts add def} def
  /k65 {/xpos xpos ppt8 add def} def
  /k6 {/xpos xpos ppt72 add def} def
  /k5 {/xpos xpos ppt66 add def} def
  /k25 {/xpos xpos ppt33 add def} def

  /showit {{/char exch def str 0 char put str ( ) eq
  {k5} {str cvx exec} ifelse} forall newline} def
  /abar {newpath xpos ppt66 add ypos moveto 0 ppt66 rlineto
  stroke closepath} def
  /acirc {newpath xpos ppt33 add ypos ppt33 add ppt33 0
  360 arc stroke closepath} def
  /bbar {newpath xpos ypos moveto 0 pts rlineto stroke
  closepath} def
```

```
/dbar {newpath xpos ppt66 add ypos moveto 0 pts rlineto
stroke closepath} def
/hcurv {newpath xpos ppt33 add ypos ppt33 add rad 180 0
arcn 0 ppt33 neg rlineto stroke closepath} def
/mbar {newpath xpos ypos moveto 0 ppt66 rlineto stroke
closepath} def

/a {abar acirc k75} def
/b {bbar acirc k75} def
/c {newpath xpos ppt33 add ypos ppt33 add rad 45 315 arc
stroke closepath k65} def
/d {acirc dbar k75} def
/e {newpath xpos ypos ppt33 add moveto ppt66 0 rlineto
xpos ppt33 add ypos ppt33 add rad 0 315 arc stroke
closepath k75} def
/f {newpath xpos ypos moveto xpos ppt33 add ypos ppt66 add
rad 180 45 arcn stroke closepath newpath xpos ypos ppt33
add moveto ppt33 0 rlineto stroke closepath k6} def
/g {newpath acirc xpos ppt66 add ypos ppt66 add moveto
xpos ppt33 add ypos rad 0 225 arcn stroke closepath k75}
def
/h {bbar hcurv k75} def
/i {mbar newpath xpos ypos pts add moveto 0 0 rlineto
stroke closepath k25} def
/j {newpath xpos ypos pts add moveto 0 0 rlineto stroke
closepath newpath xpos ypos ppt66 add moveto xpos ppt33
sub ypos
rad 0 225 arcn stroke closepath k25} def
/k {bbar newpath xpos ppt66 add ypos ppt66 add moveto
ppt66 neg ppt33 neg rlineto ppt66 ppt33 neg rlineto stroke
closepath k75} def
/l {bbar k25} def
/m {mbar hcurv k5 hcurv k75} def
/n {mbar hcurv k75} def
/o {acirc k75} def
/p {acirc newpath xpos ypos ppt33 sub moveto 0 pts rlineto
stroke closepath k75} def
/q {acirc newpath xpos ppt66 add ypos ppt33 sub moveto 0
pts rlineto stroke closepath k75} def
/r {newpath xpos ypos moveto 0 ppt66 rlineto xpos ppt33
add ypos ppt33 add rad 180 45 arcn stroke closepath k65}
def
/s {/xpos xpos ppt166 sub def newpath xpos ppt33 add ypos
ppt33 add rad 60 90 arc xpos ppt33 add ypos ppt33 add
```

```
ppt166 add ppt166 90 270 arc xpos ppt33 add ypos ppt166
add ppt166 90 270 arcn xpos ppt33 add ypos ppt33 add rad
270 240 arcn stroke closepath k6} def
/t {newpath xpos ypos ppt66 add moveto ppt33 0 rlineto
xpos ypos pts add moveto xpos ppt33 add ypos ppt33 add rad
180 315 arc stroke closepath k6} def
/u {newpath xpos ypos ppt66 add moveto xpos ppt33 add ypos
ppt33 add rad 180 360 arc stroke abar closepath k75} def
/v {newpath xpos ypos ppt66 add moveto ppt33 xpos add ypos
lineto xpos ppt66 add ypos ppt66 add lineto stroke
closepath k75} def
/w {v /xpos xpos ppt33 sub def v} def
/x {newpath xpos ypos moveto ppt66 ppt66 rlineto xpos ypos
ppt66 add moveto ppt66 ppt66 neg rlineto stroke closepath
k75} def
/y {newpath xpos ypos ppt66 add moveto xpos ppt33 add ypos
ppt33 add rad 180 360 arc xpos ppt66 add ypos ppt66 add
moveto xpos ppt33 add ypos rad 0 225 arcn stroke closepath
k75} def
/z {newpath xpos ypos ppt66 add moveto ppt66 0 rlineto
ppt66 neg dup rlineto ppt66 0 rlineto stroke k75} def
} def

650                     % top of page
7                       % weight
32                      % point size
125                     % margin
0.75 1 scale            % compress to 75%
LowerSchool             % define the characters to be used
newpage                 % set up the page from given parameters

(malcolm is tall) showit
(joan is nice) showit
(sarah can sing) showit
(geoff rides a bicycle) showit
(fiona is on holiday) showit
(barry is working) showit
(rory is old) showit
(shula is lovely) showit
(sukie is invisible) showit

showpage
```

The program requires four values on the stack, the top of page, stroke weight, point size and margin. The stroke weight should be supplied as a number between 1 and 10. A value of 1 gives a very light weight and 10 a very heavy weight.

The inter-line spacing is calculated by the **newline** procedure to be 50% of the point size. The quoted point size is the measurement in points from the top of the ascending strokes to the bottom of the character body (the base line).

To produce compressed or expanded text (in either direction), insert a line at the start of the program, scaling the x or y axis or both by a suitable amount. For example, the line:

```
0.4 1 scale
```

will produce a taller thinner version of the typeface. Note, however, that when scaling, the stroke widths will lose their regularity; verticals and horizontals will have different thicknesses depending on the direction of scaling. Further different effects can be produced by changing the line cap setting and by setting the grey level before printing text.

The program given here does not allow the use of capital letters. However, POSTSCRIPT does differentiate between upper and lower case letters in procedure (and variable) names. This means that you could expand the program to cater for capital letters by writing a short procedure for each letter. The procedure to produce A would be called **A** and so on. Go ahead!

5. THE OPERATORS

This chapter describes the syntax requirements of a POSTSCRIPT program. It also describes each of the operators in the POSTSCRIPT language. Operators are listed in alphabetical order.

SYNTAX

POSTSCRIPT programs are plain-text ASCII files with no hidden control characters or escape sequences

- Operators are delimited by any white space characters: space, tab or new-line

- User procedure and variable names are preceded by a slash character (/)

- Comments may be included following a % character. After a %, all text to the end of line is ignored.

- Strings are enclosed by parentheses ( )

- Procedures are enclosed by braces { }

- Arrays are enclosed by square brackets [ ]

- Angles are given as a number of degrees

You should also see Appendix C at the back of this book which gives limits for variable and procedure names, string lengths, integer and real numbers and so on.

OPERATORS

The first line of each entry shows the syntax of the operator. For example, the syntax line for the operator **add** is as follows:

```
num1 num2 add sum
```

The operator is shown in bold type. The stack requirements are shown to the left of the operator and the returned value of the operator (if any) is shown to the right.

In the example above, the operator **add** requires two numbers on the stack. The top two numbers are added together and the sum is placed on top of the stack.

Putting some real numbers into this example, a program containing the line:

```
3.4 5.6 add
```

would take the numbers 3.4 and 5.6, add them together and place the sum (9.0) on the stack.

Any syntax line which contains a hyphen on either side of the operator indicates that either nothing is required from the stack or nothing is returned to the stack. For example, the **showpage** operator has the syntax line:

```
- showpage -
```

This operator prints out the current page. Nothing is required from the stack and nothing is returned to the stack after the operation.

OPERANDS

The various types of operators require different types of operands. The conventions used in this book to refer to real numbers, integers, strings booleans and other objects are as follows:

r, x, y, x1, y1 etc	real numbers
num1, num2	real numbers
int1, int2	integers
any1 any2	any of the above
string1, string2	strings (always in brackets)
angle1, angle2	angles in degrees
bool	boolean (true or false)
object1, object2	any of the above
array1, array2	one dimensional arrays
packedarray1, packedarray2	packed arrays
dict1, dict2	dictionaries
key	dictionary item
value	value of a dictionary item
font	name of a font
matrix1, matrix2	matrices

Note: The bar character, 'l', is used to represent the bottom of the operand stack.

THE OPERATORS

=

---

object1 = -

Removes the top item from the stack and prints a text representation of that item to the standard output file. Takes any type of operand.

See also: ==, **clear, pstack, stack.**

==

---

object1 == -

Removes the top item from the stack and prints a text representation of that item to the standard output file. This operator attempts to print the operand in a form as close as possible to the form the operand took when it was added to the stack. Therefore strings are enclosed in parentheses, arrays in brackets and so on. Takes any type of operand.

See also: =, **clear, pstack, stack.**

[

- [mark

The operator [(or its synonym **mark**) places a mark on the stack which can be used as a separator or pointer. The stack may contain any number of **marks** at one time.

See also:], **cleartomark, counttomark, mark.**

]

---

mark object0 object1... objectn-1] array

Used as the end marker when creating an array. The operator **mark** (or its synonym [) is used to start the definition, followed by n objects of any type and the operator]. Arrays can contain a mixture of object types.

See also: [, **array, astore, mark.**

---

abs

> num1 **abs** num2

Removes the top number from the stack and returns the absolute value of that number to the stack. The type of num2 is the same as num1.

See also: **neg**.

---

add

> num1 num2 **add** sum

Removes the top two numbers from the stack, adds them together and returns the sum of the two numbers to the stack. If both num1 and num2 are integers and the sum is within the allowed integer range, then the returned value is an integer, otherwise the returned value is a real number.

See also: **div, idiv, mul, sub**.

---

aload

> array **aload** array0 array1... arrayn-1 array

> packedarray **aload** packedarray0 packedarray1... packedarrayn-1 packedarray

Pushes the value of all n elements of the array or packed array onto the stack and finally pushes the array object itself onto the stack.

See also: **astore, get, getinterval**.

---

anchorsearch

> string1 substring1 **anchorsearch** (if found) end match true

> string1 substring1 **anchorsearch** (if not found) string false

Compares substring1 with the start of string1. If substring1 is not longer than string1 and it matches the first characters of string1 then the end of string1 (after the matching characters) is placed on the stack followed by the matching portion and a boolean true.

If substring1 is longer than string1 or it does not match the start of string1 then string is placed on the stack followed by a boolean false.

See also: **search, token.**

---

and

booll bool2 **and** bool3

int1 int2 **and** int3

If the operands are boolean, the logical conjunction of the two cases is returned to the stack. If the operands are integers, the bitwise **and** of their binary representations is placed on the stack.

See also: **false, not, or, true, xor.**

---

arc

x y rad angle1 angle2 **arc** -

Appends an arc anticlockwise to the current graphics path using centre co-ordinates x, y, with a radius rad starting at angle1 and ending at angle2. If there is already a current point in the current path a straight line is drawn from the current point to the start of the arc.

Curves are drawn to a circular path from the positive x axis of the xy co-ordinate system. If the **scale** operator has been used to produce non-linear scaling, the resulting arc will be elliptical.

See also: **arcn, arcto, curveto, scale.**

---

arcn

x y rad angle1 angle2 **arcn** -

Appends an arc clockwise to the current graphics path using centre co- ordinates x, y, with a radius rad starting at angle1 and ending at angle2. If there is already a current point in the current path a straight line is drawn from the current point to the start of the arc.

Curves are drawn to a circular path from the positive x axis of the xy co-ordinate system. If the **scale** operator has been used to produce non-linear scaling, the resulting arc will be elliptical.

See also: **arc, arcto, curveto, scale.**

arcto

x1 y1 x2 y2 r **arcto** xt1 yt1 xt2 yt2

Appends an arc to the current path possibly preceded by a straight line tangential to the arc and joining the current point to the beginning of the arc. The arc is drawn on the inner angle formed by, and tangentially to, a line between the current point and x1, y1 and a line from x1, y1 to x2, y2.

Four values are returned by this operator; these are the x and y co-ordinates of the two tangent points.

See also: **arc, arcn, curveto.**

array

int1 **array** array

Initiates an array of int1 elements. On initialisation, each element consists of only a null object. Arrays may contain any POSTSCRIPT object. The value of int1 must not be greater than 65535, the maximum number of elements allowed in an array.

See also: **[,], aload, astore, packedarray.**

ashow

num1 num2 string **ashow** -

Prints a string in a similar manner to **show**. The difference is that the value of num1 is added to the current x position after each character and the value of num2 to the current y position after each character.

See also: **awidthshow, kshow, show, widthshow.**

astore

object0 object1... objectn-1 n **astore** array

Takes n off the stack followed by n objects. These objects are stored into an array of n elements. The topmost object on the stack becomes element n-1 of the array and the bottommost object becomes element 0. The complete array is placed on the stack.

See also: **aload, put, putinterval.**

---

atan

numerator denominator **atan** angle

Removes the top two numbers from the stack and returns the angle (in degrees) whose tangent is numerator/denominator.

See also: **cos, sin.**

---

awidthshow

x1 y1 char x2 y2 string **awidthshow** -

Combines the operators **ashow** and **widthshow** to print string with the values of x1 and y1 added to the current point co-ordinates after each character. Also, the values of x2 and y2 are added to the current point co-ordinates after any occurrences of the specified character char. This allows selective spacing adjustment on certain characters in a string - often the space character when justifying text.

See also: **ashow, kshow, show, widthshow.**

---

banddevice

matrix wid ht proc **banddevice** -

Used to specify a band buffer as the raster memory used when building a page image. The page is defined as 8 x wid pixels wide and 8 x ht pixels high. The matrix operand defines the default transformation matrix for the page. The proc operand specifies a procedure to be executed as part of the process of printing a page with the operators **showpage** and **copypage.**

Not all POSTSCRIPT devices use band buffers and so not all POSTSCRIPT devices will support this operator.

See also: **copypage, framedevice, nulldevice, renderbands, showpage.**

---

begin

dict **begin** -

Places dict on top of the dictionary stack, making dict the current dictionary.

See also: **countdictstack, dictstack, end.**

---
bind
---

proc **bind** proc

Replaces each operator in the procedure proc with its executable value, 'binding' the procedure into an unchangeable, executable form. This process is rather like taking a text program for a computer language and compiling it into its executable form.

Using **bind** has two effects; 1. the procedure is given a fixed executable form which remains constant, even if procedures or variables which occur within the named procedure are later defined. 2. The execution speed of the named procedure is increased as each operator is no longer looked-up at execution time, being already in its executable form.

See also: **load.**

---
bitshift
---

int1 int2 **bitshift** int3

Shifts the binary representation of the integer int1 by int2 bits. Positive values of int2 effect a left shift; negative values a right shift. Both operands must be integers. For right shift operations, int1 must be positive.

See also: **and, not, or, xor.**

---
bytesavailable
---

file **bytesavailable** int

This operator takes the name of a valid open file from the stack and returns to the stack the number of bytes which are available for reading without any wait time. A returned value of -1 indicates that either the end of file has been reached or that the number of bytes available cannot be determined for some other reason.

See also: **read, readhexstring, readline, readstring.**

---
cachestatus

- **cachestatus** bitsize bitmax matsize matmax charsize charmax bytlimit

Returns information on the font cache memory usage. The returned values have the following meanings:

bitsize	bitmap bytes used
bitmax	bitmap bytes maximum
matsize	font/matrix bytes used
matmax	font/matrix bytes maximum
charsize	total cached characters
charmax	maximum cached characters
bytlimit	maximum bytes per character

The first six returned values are for information only. The last, bytlimit, can be changed by using the operator **setcachelimit**.

See also: **setcachelimit**.

ceiling

num1 **ceiling** num2

Removes the top number from the stack and returns the lowest integer which is greater than or equal to num1.

See also: **floor, truncate, cvi**.

charpath

string bool **charpath** -

Appends an outline to the current path which takes the form of the path of the characters in string. The bool operand is concerned with one of the definitions for the current font dictionary.

A full explanation of font dictionaries is beyond the scope of this book. However, some fonts are designed to be stroked rather than filled or outlined. Others are designed to be filled or clipped but not stroked. If bool is false, the resulting path may be stroked only. If bool is true, the resulting path may be filled or clipped but not stroked. See the example program in chapter 2 under the heading GRAY, OUTLINE AND CLIPPED TEXT for further details.

See also: **clip, flattenpath, pathbbox, show**.

clear

lobject1... objectn **clear** -

Removes all objects from the stack and discards them, leaving the stack clear.

See also: **cleartomark, count, pop.**

cleartomark

mark object1... objectn **cleartomark** -

Repeatedly removes objects from the stack and discards them until a mark is detected. This too is removed from the stack and discarded.

See also: **clear, counttomark, mark, pop.**

clip

- **clip** -

The default clipping path is the limits of user space, but this may be clipped to another, smaller area by using the **clip** operator. After specifying a path, use of the **clip** operator makes the new clipping path any area that is within both the old and the new paths.

A new clipping path may not be explicitly reset to its previous path following the use of clip. However, the **gsave** and **grestore** operators may be used to enclose a clipping action, allowing you to return to the previous clipping path.

See also: **clippath, eoclip, grestore, gsave, initclip.**

clippath

- **clippath** -

Sets the current path to accord with the current clipping path. This may be used to determine the exact extent and nature of the current clipping path.

See also: **clip, eoclip, initclip.**

closefile

file **closefile** -

Closes the named file. The association between the file object and the file itself is then terminated. When the named file is an output file, any buffered characters are directed to that file immediately before the file is closed (see **flushfile**). Other actions may be performed according to the device in use.

See also: **file, flushfile, read, status.**

closepath

- **closepath** -

Closes the current path by appending a line joining the current point to the starting point of the path.

See also: **clip, fill, stroke.**

concat

matrix **concat** -

Concatenates the current transformation matrix (CTM) with the given matrix. This can be used to combine a **scale, rotate** and **translate** into one operation.

See also: **concatmatrix, matrix, rotate, scale, setmatrix, translate.**

concatmatrix

matrix1 matrix2 matrix3 **concatmatrix** matrix3

Concatenates the contents of matrix1 and matrix2 and places the result in matrix3. The modified matrix3 is returned to the stack. This operator has no effect on the current transformation matrix (CTM).

See also: **concat, matrix, rotate, scale, setmatrix, translate.**

copy

object1... objectn n **copy** object1... objectn object1... objectn

array1 array2 **copy** subarray1

dict1 dict2 **copy** dict2

packedarray1 array1 **copy** subarray1

string1 string2 **copy** substring1

In the first example, when n is a positive integer, **copy** makes a copy of the topmost n objects on the stack and places them on top of the stack. Otherwise, the contents of the first composite object are copied into the second. The operands of the composite objects must be the same, except in the case of packed arrays. The **copy** operator copies the value of the stacked objects, not the objects themselves.

See also: **dup.**

---

copypage

- **copypage** -

Causes the output device to print one copy of the current page without erasing the current page or changing the graphics state (current point, gray level, line width etc).

More than one copy can be produced by **copypage** and **showpage**, by redefining the value of the internal variable #copies. For example, to produce 10 printed copies for each use of **copypage** or **showpage**, use the program line:

```
/#copies 10 def
```

See also: **showpage, erasepage.**

---

cos

angle1 **cos** num1

Removes the top number from the stack and returns the cosine of that angle. The angle should be a number of degrees.

See also: **atan, sin.**

---

count

lobject1... objectn **count** lobject1... objectn n

Counts the number of objects on the stack and places the count on top of the stack.

See also: **counttomark.**

countdictstack

- **countdictstack** integer1

Counts the number of dictionaries on the dictionary stack and places the count on top of the operand stack.

See also: **begin, dictstack, end.**

countexecstack

- **countexecstack** integer1

Counts the number of objects on the execution stack and places the count on top of the operand stack.

See also: **execstack.**

counttomark

mark object1... objectn **counttomark** mark object1... objectn n

Counts the number of objects on the stack down to any **mark** and places the count on top of the stack. The **mark** is not included in the count.

See also: **count, mark.**

currentcacheparams

- **currentcacheparams** mark thresh max

Places a **mark** on the stack followed by the threshold and maximum cache parameters. The number of parameters may change in late implementations of the language. See **setcacheparams** for further details.

See also: **setcacheparams.**

currentdash

- **currentdash** array offset

Places on the stack the current dash array and the dash pattern offset. See **setdash** for further details.

See also: **setdash, stroke.**

---
currentdict

- **currentdict** dict

Places on the operator stack a copy of the top element on the dictionary stack, ie, the current dictionary.

See also: **begin, dictstack.**

---
currentfile

- **currentfile** file

Returns the name of the current input file to the operand stack. The default input filename is **-filestream-**.

See also: **exec, run.**

---
currentflat

- **currentflat** num1

Returns the current flatness setting in the graphics state. See **setflat** for further details.

See also: **flattenpath, setflat.**

---
currentfont

- **currentfont** font

Returns to the stack the name of the current font dictionary.

See also: **setfont.**

---
currentgray

- **currentgray** num1

Returns to the stack the gray setting of the current color in the graphics state. If the current colour has a hue in addition to the gray setting, the value of the colour brightness is returned.

See also: **currenthsbcolor, currentrgbcolor, setgray.**

---

currenthsbcolor

- **currenthsbcolor** hue saturation brightness

Returns the hue, saturation and brightness levels (real numbers) of the current colour setting in the graphics state.

See also: **currentgray, currentrgbcolor, setgray, sethsbcolor, setrgbcolor.**

---

currentlinecap

- **currentlinecap** int1

Returns to the stack the current value of the line cap setting in the graphics state.

See also: **currentlinejoin, setlinecap.**

---

currentlinejoin

- **currentlinejoin** int1

Returns to the stack the value of the current line join setting in the graphics state.

See also: **currentlinecap, setlinejoin.**

---

currentlinewidth

- **currentlinewidth** n

Returns to the stack the value of the current line width setting in the graphics state. The line width is specified as n/72 inches.

See also: **setlinewidth.**

---

currentmatrix

matrix **currentmatrix** matrix

Takes a matrix off the stack and replaces its value with that of the current transformation matrix (CTM) in the graphics state. The modified version of the matrix is placed on the stack.

See also: **defaultmatrix, initmatrix, rotate, scale, setmatrix, translate.**

currentmiterlimit

- **currentmiterlimit** num1

Returns to the stack the value of the current mitre limit setting in the graphics state.

See also: **setmiterlimit**.

currentpacking

- **currentpacking** bool

Returns to the stack a boolean which indicates the current array packing mode.

See also: **packedarray, setpacking.**

currentpoint

- **currentpoint** x y

Returns to the stack the x and y co-ordinates of the current point in the graphics state. If no current point is set then the **nocurrentpoint** error is generated.

See also: **arc, curveto, lineto, moveto.**

currentrgbcolor

- **currentrgbcolor** red green blue

Returns to the stack the current values (real numbers) of the red, green and blue colour settings in the graphics state.

See also: **currentgray, currenthsbcolor, setrgbcolor.**

currentscreen

- **currentscreen** freq angle proc

Returns the current values of the halftone screen setting in the graphics state.

See also: **currenttransfer, setscreen.**

currenttransfer

- **currenttransfer** proc

Returns the current transfer function operating in the graphics state.

See also: **currentscreen, settransfer.**

curveto

x1 y1 x2 y2 x3 y3 **curveto** -

Appends a curve to the current path. The curve takes the form of a Bézier cubic section. A full explanation of this geometric form is beyond the scope of this book, however, the following may be useful:

- the current point is x0,y0
- the curve starts tangential to the line x0,y0 - x1,y1
- the curve ends tangential to the line x2y2 - x3y3
- the curve is entirely enclosed by a convex quadrilateral defined by the four points x0y0, x1y1, x2y2, x3y3, x4y4.

See also the section headed USING CURVETO in chapter 3.

See also: **arc, arcn, arcto, lineto, moveto, rcurveto.**

cvi

number **cvi** int1

string **cvi** int1

Converts either a real number or a string to an integer. Given a real number, the operator truncates any fractional part of the number and converts it to an integer. Given a string representation of a real number or integer, the operator converts the string to an integer. The result is returned to the stack.

See also: **cvlit, cvn, cvr, cvrs, cvs, cvx.**

cvlit

any **cvlit** any

Converts the object on the top of the stack to is literal rather than executable form.

See also: **cvi, cvn, cvr, cvrs, cvs, cvx.**

---

cvn

string **cvn** name

Converts the string on the top of the stack to a name object.

See also: **cvi, cvlit, cvr, cvrs, cvs, cvx.**

---

cvr

integer **cvr** number

string **cvr** number

Converts either an integer or a string to a real number. Given an integer, the operator simply converts it to a real number. Given a string representation of a number, the operator converts that string to a real number.

See also: **cvi, cvlit, cvn, cvrs, cvs, cvx.**

---

cvrs

number base stringname **cvrs** string

Converts a base 10 number into a string representation of that number in a given base. The resulting string is assigned to a named variable and the substring used is placed on the stack.

The given base may be in the range 2 to 36. In the returned string, digits greater than 9 are represented by the letters A to Z.

See also: **cvi, cvlit, cvn, cvr, cvs, cvx.**

---

cvs

any string **cvs** substring

Converts any object into its string representation, which is then stored in a named string. The substring actually used is placed on the stack.

If the given object is other than a number, string, boolean, operator or name, the string '--nostringval--' is returned.

See also: **cvi, cvlit, cvn, cvr, cvrs, cvx.**

---

cvx

any **cvx** any

Converts the top object on the stack into its executable rather than its literal form.

See also: **cvi, cvlit, cvn, cvr, cvrs, cvs.**

---

def

key value **def** -

Assigns value to key in the current dictionary. If the named key already exists in the current dictionary, its value is changed to the given value.

See also: **put, store.**

---

defaultmatrix

matrix **defaultmatrix** matrix

Replaces the value of the given matrix with the default transformation matrix. This new version of the given matrix is then placed on the stack.

See also: **currentmatrix, initmatrix, setmatrix.**

---

definefont

key font **definefont** font

Makes the given font available as a read-only font dictionary associated with the given key in the overall font dictionary.

See also: **makefont, scalefont, setfont.**

---

dict

int1 **dict** dict

Creates an empty dictionary with a capacity of int1 elements (int1 must be positive). The empty, created dictionary is then placed on the operand stack.

See also: **begin, end, length, maxlength.**

dictstack

array **dictstack** subarray

Stores copies of all the dictionaries on the dictionary stack into the given array (n elements). The initial subarray of array is then placed on the stack. Element 0 of the subarray contains the bottommost dictionary and element n-1 contains the topmost dictionary.

See also: **countdictstack**.

div

num1 num2 **div** num3

Removes the two operands from the stack and divides num1 by num2. The real number result is placed on the stack.

See also: **add, idiv, mod, mul, sub.**

dtransform

dvecx dvecy **dtransform** dvecx' dvecy'

dvecx dvecy matrix **dtransform** dvecx' dvecy'

The first example transforms the CTM by the given distance vector (dvecx, dvecy). The resulting distance vector corresponds to device space. The second example transforms the given matrix by the given distance vector.

See also: **idtransform, itransform, transform.**

dup

object **dup** object object

Duplicates the topmost object on the stack. The values of copied composite objects such as arrays are shared between the copies.

See also: **copy, index.**

echo

bool **echo** -

Specifies the echoing of characters to the standard output file when received from the standard input file. Equates to ECHO ON or OFF in a communications system.

See also: **file.**

end

- end -

Removes the current (i.e. topmost) dictionary from the dictionary stack and discards it. The next dictionary on the stack becomes the current dictionary.

See also: **begin, countdictstack, dictstack.**

eoclip

- eoclip -

Sets the current clipping path to the current path. The 'insideness' is determined by the even-odd rule, rather than the default non-zero rule. This operator has the same effect as **clip** with the exception of the way the inside of a path is determined.

See also: **clip, clippath, eofill, initclip.**

eofill

- eofill -

Fills the inside of the current path with the current colour. The 'insideness' is determined by the even-odd rule, rather than the default non-zero rule. This operator has the same effect as **fill** with the exception of the way the inside of a path is determined.

eq

object1 object2 **eq** bool

Removes the top two objects from the stack. If the two are equal, a boolean true is placed on the stack. Otherwise a boolean false is placed on the stack. Note that distinct arrays, despite being equal in size and content, are considered unequal.

See also: **ge, gt, le, lt, ne.**

---

erasepage

- erasepage -

Erases the entire current page by filling with gray level 1. The current graphics state is not affected and no page is printed out.

See also: **copypage, fill, showpage.**

---

errordict

- **errordict** dict

Places the dictionary object errordict on the operand stack. **errordict** is the key name in systemdict associated with the errordict object.

See also: **systemdict, userdict.**

---

exch

object1 object2 **exch** object2 object1

Exchanges the positions of the top two items on the stack.

See also: **index, roll.**

---

exec

object **exec** -

Causes the top object on the stack to be executed as if it were received directly from the current input file as part of a program. If the top object is not executable, that object is returned unaltered to the stack.

See also: **cvx, run, xcheck.**

---

execstack

array **execstack** subarray

Stores all unexecuted material (for example, an object made executable by **cvx** but not yet executed) into the named array. The subarray containing the material is then placed on the operand stack.

See also: **exec, countexecstack, cvx.**

executive

Note: this is not an operator, but may be used in programs or directly in real-time communications to enter POSTSCRIPT interactive mode. See appendix B, EXECUTIVE Mode for a full description of POSTSCRIPT's interactive mode.

executeonly

array **executeonly** array

file **executeonly** file

packearray **executeonly** packearray

string **executeonly** string

Takes an array, file, packed array or string from the stack and converts it into an execute-only object. This means that after conversion, the object may not be accessed in any way other than to be executed.

See also: **rcheck, readonly, noaccess, wcheck, xcheck.**

exit

- **exit** -

Exits from the most recent repeating program structure (**for, forall, loop, pathforall, repeat, renderbands**). Operand and dictionary stacks are unaffected. Program execution continues at the first object after the close of the repeating structure just exited.

If there is no current repeating program structure an error is returned.

See also: **stop.**

exp

base exponent **exp** number

Raises the given base to the power of exponent. The resulting real number is then placed on the stack. If exponent has a fractional part, it must be positive or an non-valid result will be returned.

See also: **ln, log, mul, sqrt.**

false

- **false** false

Places a boolean false on the stack. This object can then be tested by various POSTSCRIPT operators.

See also: **and, not, or, true, xor.**

file

string1 string2 **file** file

Creates and opens a file, identified by string1, as an input or output file as identified by string 2 according to the following:

string2	file type
(r)	Read only (input)
(w)	Write only (output)

The file object is placed on the operand stack. The file is automatically closed by **closefile,** by an end-of-file marker or by restoring a state which was saved before the file was opened.

See also: **closefile, currentfile, read, status, write.**

fill

- **fill** -

Fills the area enclosed by the current path with the current colour. The colour may be considered as an opaque medium. Whatever the current colour, even white, the background is obscured by filling, or printing over it. The **fill** operator automatically closes any currently open path and carries out a **newpath** after the fill.

See also: **clip, eoclip, eofill, stroke.**

findfont

fontname **findfont** font

Finds the font identified by fontname and places it on the stack. This is a composite POSTSCRIPT item, not an operator. It can be redefined according to the software or hardware needs of your POSTSCRIPT device.

See also: **definefont, FontDirectory, makefont, scalefont, setfont.**

flattenpath

- flattenpath -

Replaces all parts of the current path created with the **curveto** operator with approximations made from short, straight line path segments. The accuracy of the approximation depends upon the **currentflat** setting. A **flattenpath** is carried out implicitly during stroke and fill operations, again referring to the **currentflat** setting.

See also: **currentflat, curveto, pathbbox, setflat.**

floor

num1 **floor** num2

Rounds the value of num1 down to the next whole number and returns the new value to the stack. Values below zero are rounded down (away from zero). For example:

```
-6.7 floor
```

returns the value -7.0. The type of the number returned is the same as that of the operand.

See also: **ceiling, round, truncate.**

flush

- flush -

Sends any buffered characters directly to the standard output file.

See also: **flushfile, print.**

flushfile

file **flushfile** -

If the named file is an output file, **flushfile** sends any buffered characters directly to that file. If the named file is an input file, all data up to the next end-of-file marker is ignored. This operator can be used in user-generated error handling routines.

See also: **flush, read, write.**

FontDirectory

- **FontDirectory** dict

(Note that the capital letters are significant). Places the global font dictionary onto the stack. Entries are made in this dictionary with **definefont** and read with **findfont**. Some implementations of POSTSCRIPT may allow access to fonts (via **findfont**) which do not appear in the global font dictionary.

See also: **definefont, findfont.**

for

start increment end proc **for** -

Executes the given procedure once for each value between start and end in increment steps. If the given procedure does not use the values placed for it on the stack, the numbers will accumulate there.

The looping structure may be terminated by use of the **exit** operator.

See also: **exit, forall, loop, pathforall, repeat.**

forall

array proc **forall** -

dict proc **forall** -

packedarray proc **forall** -

string proc **forall** -

Places each element of the first operand on the stack and execues the named procedure once for each element. In the case of a string, the elements placed on the stack are the ASCII values for each character - not the characters themselves. Note that if the named procedure does not remove the elements from the stack they will accumulate there.

See also: **exit, for, loop, pathforall, repeat.**

---

framedevice

matrix wid ht proc **framedevice** -

This is a hardware dependent operator and is not available in all implementations of POSTSCRIPT. Creates a frame buffer as the output device. The output buffer operates as raster memory. The buffer is 8 x wid pixels wide by ht pixels high. The current clipping path in the graphics state is determined by ht, wid and matrix. Proc is executed during the actions of **copypage** and **showpage** and transmits the contents of the frame buffer to the output device.

See also: **banddevice, copypage, nulldevice, showpage.**

---

ge

num1 num2 **ge** bool

string1 string2 **ge** bool

Removes the top two objects from the stack and compares them. If the first (bottommost) object is greater than or equal to the second then a boolean true is placed on the stack, otherwise a boolean false is placed on the stack.

See also: **eq, gt, le, lt, ne.**

---

get

array index **get** any

dict index **get** any

packedarray index **get** any

string index **get** int

Gets an element indicated by index, from the given array, dictionary, packed array or string. The element is placed on the stack. In the case of a string, the element is the ASCII value of the specified character, not the character itself.

If the first operand is a dictionary, **get** expects index to be a key from that dictionary. The value associated with that key is returned to the stack.

See also: **getinterval, put, putinterval.**

getinterval

array index count **getinterval** subarray

packedarray index count **getinterval** subarray

string index count **getinterval** substring

Creates an array, packed array or string which contains count elements starting at index in the given array, packed array or string. Count must be a positive integer such that count + index does not exceed the length of the first operand.

See also: **get, put, putinterval.**

grestore

- grestore -

Restores the previously **gsaved** graphics state from the graphics state stack. That graphics state is then removed from the graphics state stack. If no graphics state was saved, the default graphics state is restored and the graphics state stack is unaffected.

See also: **grestoreall, gsave.**

grestoreall

- grestoreall -

Repeatedly removes previously **gsaved** graphics states from the graphics state stack until either the bottommost state is found and restored (but not removed from the stack), or a graphics state is found which was saved with **save** not **gsave**. This state is restored and again left on the graphics state stack.

See also: **grestore, gsave, restore, save.**

gsave

- gsave -

Places a copy of the current graphics state on the graphics state stack. This state may later be restored by using the **grestore** operator.

See also: **grestore, grestoreall, restore, save.**

---

gt

num1 num2 **gt** bool

string1 string2 **gt** bool

Removes the top two objects from the stack and compares them. If the first (bottommost) object is greater than the second then a boolean true is placed on the stack, otherwise a boolean false is placed on the stack.

See also: **eq, ge, le, lt, ne.**

---

identmatrix

matrix **identmatrix** matrix

Removes the matrix from the stack and replaces its value with the identity matrix, [1.0 0.0 0.0 1.0 0.0 0.0]. This matrix transforms any given coordinate back to itself. The identity matrix is then placed on the stack.

See also: **currentmatrix, defaultmatrix, initmatrix, matrix.**

---

idiv

int1 int2 **idiv** int3

Removes the two integers from the stack, divides int1 by int 2 and places the integral part of the result on the stack.

See also: **add, cvi, div, mod, mul, sub.**

---

idtransform

dvecx' dvecy' **idtransform** dvecx dvecy

dvecx' dvecy' matrix **idtransform** dvecx dvecy

The first example transforms the device space distance vector dvecx' dvecy' by the inverse of the current transformation matrix. The result, a distance vector in user space, is placed on the stack. In the second example, the same process is carried out, but using the given matrix rather than the current transformation matrix. This process is the inverse of that carried out by **dtransform**.

See also: **currentmatrix, dtransform, itransform, transform.**

if

bool proc **if** -

If the boolean is true, the procedure is executed. If the boolean is false, the procedure is not executed and program execution continues at the statement after the **if** operator.

See also: **ifelse.**

ifelse

bool proc1 proc2 **ifelse** -

If the boolean is true, proc1 is executed. If the boolean is false, proc2 is executed. In either case, program execution continues at the statement after the **ifelse** operator.

See also: **if.**

image

wid ht bits-per-pixel matrix proc **image** -

Renders a bitmapped image of a given width and height (in pixels) using a given number of bits per pixel to produce 2, 4, 16 or 256 levels of gray per pixel. The given matrix maps the data into device space. The given procedure reads the image data. See the description on the **image** and **imagemask** operators in chapter 3.

See also: **imagemask.**

imagemask

wid ht bool matrix proc **imagemask** -

Renders a bitmapped image of a given width and height (in pixels) using either 1's to paint black pixels (bool = true) or 0's to paint black pixels (bool = false). The given matrix maps the data into device space. The given procedure reads the image data. See the description on the **image** and **imagemask** operators in chapter 3.

See also: **image.**

index

objectn... object0 n **index** objectn... object0 objectn

Takes a positive integer, n, off the stack and gets the nth object from the top of the stack (counting from 0) and places a copy of that object on the stack.

See also: **copy, dup, roll.**

initclip

- **initclip** -

Restores the current clipping path in the graphics state with the default device clipping path - usually the maximum image area for the output device.

See also: **clip, clippath, eoclip, initgraphics.**

initgraphics

- **initgraphics** -

Resets a number of the graphics state functions to their default condition. This operator has the same effect as the following sequence of commands:

```
initmatrix newpath initclip [] 0 setdash
0 setgray 0 setlinecap 0 setlinejoin
1 setlinewidth 10 setmiterlimit
```

See also: **grestoreall, restore.**

initmatrix

- **initmatrix** -

Resets the current transformation matrix to the default transformation matrix for the output device.

See also: **currentmatrix, defaultmatrix, setmatrix.**

invertmatrix

matrix1 matrix2 **invertmatrix** matrix2

Removes both matrices from the stack and gives matrix2 the value of the inverse of matrix1. That is, if matrix1 transforms a coordinate from xy to x'y', matrix2 transforms x'y' to xy. The modified version of matrix2 is placed on the stack.

See also: **idtransform, itransform.**

itransform

x' y' **itransform** x y

x' y' matrix **itransform** x y

The first example transforms the device space coordinate x' y' by the inverse of the current transformation matrix. The result, a coordinate in user space, is placed on the stack. In the second example, the same process is carried out, but using the inverse of the given matrix rather than the current transformation matrix.

See also: **currentmatrix, idtransform, invertmatrix, itransform, transform.**

known

dict key **known** bool

Removes the two operands from the stack. If the given key is found in the given dictionary, a boolean true is placed on the stack. If no such key is found in dict, a false is placed on the stack.

See also: **get, load, where.**

kshow

proc string **kshow** -

Allows strings to be printed character by character with the execution of a user procedure between the characters. **kshow** prints a character, updates the current point by the width of that character and places its ASCII value on the stack. The ASCII value of the next character is also placed on the stack. (The ASCII values are stacked as integers). The given procedure is then executed. This allows the procedure to examine the character just printed and the one which is about to be printed and take some appropriate action.

If the user procedure does not remove the ASCII codes from the stack during its execution, they will accumulate there.

See also: **ashow, awidthshow, show, widthshow.**

le

num1 num2 **le** bool

string1 string2 **le** bool

Removes both operands from the stack and compares them. If the first operand is less than or equal to the second, a boolean true is placed on the stack. If the second is greater than the first, a boolean false is placed on the stack.

In the case of strings, the ASCII codes of the characters in each string are compared.

See also: **eq, ge, gt, lt, ne.**

length

array **length** int

dict **length** int

packedarray **length** int

string **length** int

Removes the operand from the stack and returns the number of elements in its value. This integer is placed on the stack.

See also: **array, dict, maxlength, string.**

lineto

x y **lineto** -

Removes the two operands from the stack and appends a straight line segment to the the current path. The line joins the current point and x y in user space.

See also: **arc, arcn, closepath, curveto, moveto, rlineto, rmoveto.**

ln

num1 **ln** num2

Removes the operand from the stack and returns to the stack its natural logarithm. The result is a real number.

See also: **exp, log.**

load

key **load** value

Searches each dictionary on the dictionary stack for the given key. If the key is found, its associated value is placed on the stack. If the returned key value is executable, that object is **not** automatically executed.

See also: **get, where.**

log

number1 **log** number2

Removes the operand from the stack and returns to the stack its base 10 logarithm. The result is a real number.

See also: **exp, ln.**

loop

proc **loop** -

Repeats execution of the given procedure until the **exit** or **stop** operators are encountered. In the case of **exit**, program execution then continues at the point following the **loop** operator. If neither **exit** nor **stop** is encountered, the procedure loops indefinitely. This may only be stopped by an external interrupt.

See also: **exit, for, forall, interrupt, pathforall, repeat.**

lt

num1 num2 **lt** bool

string1 string2 **lt** bool

Removes both operands from the stack and compares them. If the first operand is less than the second, a boolean true is placed on the stack. Otherwise a boolean false is placed on the stack.

In the case of strings, the ASCII codes of the characters in each string are compared.

See also: **eq, ge, gt, lt, ne.**

---
makefont
---

font1 matrix **makefont** font2

Removes the two operands from the stack and applies matrix to the given font to produce font2. This modified version of font1 is placed on the stack.

---
mark

- **mark** mark

The operator **mark** (or its synonym [) places a mark on the stack which can be used as a separator or pointer. The stack may contain any number of marks at one time.

See also:], **cleartomark, counttomark, mark.**

---
matrix

- **matrix** matrix

Creates a POSTSCRIPT identity matrix and places it on the stack. The identity matrix contains [1.0 0.0 0.0 1.0 0.0 0.0] and maps points directly onto themselves.

See also: **array, currentmatrix, defaultmatrix, initmatrix, setmatrix.**

---
maxlength
---

dict **maxlength** int

Returns the maximum number of entries that the given dictionary may hold.

See also: **dict, length.**

---
mod
---

int1 int2 **mod** int3

Removes the two operands from the stack and divides int1 by int2. The remainder from the division (an integer) is placed on the stack. The result has the same sign as int1.

See also: **div, idiv.**

moveto

x y **moveto** -

Sets the current point to x y, starting a new sub-path of the current path in the graphics state.

See also: **arc, arcn, closepath, curveto, lineto, rlineto, rmoveto.**

mul

num1 num2 **mul** num3

Takes the two operands off the stack and multiplies them, returning the product of the two numbers to the stack. If both of the numbers are integers and the product lies within POSTSCRIPT's integer limits, the result is an integer. Otherwise the result is a real number.

See also: **add, div, idiv, mod, sub.**

ne

any1 any2 **ne** bool

Removes the two operands from the stack and compares them. If they are not equal, a boolean true is placed on the stack. Otherwise a boolean false is placed on the stack. Note that distinct arrays, despite being equal in size and content, are considered unequal.

See also: **eq, ge, gt, le, lt.**

neg

num1 **neg** num2

Removes the operand from the stack and negates it, placing the new value on the stack. The type of num2 is the same as num1 except in the case of POSTSCRIPT's most negative integer, when num2 is a real.

See also: **abs.**

newpath

- newpath -

Re-initialises the current path to be empty. The current point is therefore undefined after the use of **newpath**.

See also: **currentpoint, moveto, rmoveto.**

noaccess

array **noaccess** array

dict **noaccess** dict

file **noaccess** file

packedarray **noaccess** packedarray

string **noaccess** string

Causes the given object to become unavailable to access by a POSTSCRIPT program. The use of this operator is internal to POSTSCRIPT.

See also: **executeonly, rcheck, readonly, wcheck, xcheck.**

not

bool1 **not** bool2

int1 **not** int2

Given a boolean, **not** returns the logical negation of that boolean; given an integer, **not** returns the one's compliment of that integer.

See also: **and, if, or, xor.**

null

- null null

Places a null object onto the operand stack. (Note: a null object, not the **null** operator itself.)

See also: **type.**

nulldevice

- nulldevice -

Installs the null device as the current output device. This means that any operations which would ordinarily render marks onto the paper, have no effect. However, the null device otherwise operates in the same way as any physical output device; fonts are cached and the graphics state is manipulated in the usual way.

nulldevice also sets a clipping path to a single point at the origin and sets the default transformation matrix to [1.0 0.0 0.0 1.0 0.0 0.0]. The use of this operator should be carried out between the **gsave** and **grestore** operators so that its effects may be cancelled.

See also: **banddevice, framedevice, grestore, gsave.**

or

bool1 bool2 **or** bool3

int1 int2 **or** int3

Given two booleans, **or** returns the result of a logical **or** on the two objects; given two integers, **or** returns the bitwise inclusive **or** of their binary representations.

See also: **and, not, xor.**

packedarray

obj0 obj1... objn-1 n **packedarray** packedarray

Takes the integer n off the stack, and creates a packed array object of n elements. The next n objects from the stack are placed into the packed array which is then itself placed on the stack. The resulting packed array has read-only access.

See also: **aload, currentpacking, setpacking.**

pathbbox

- pathbbox x1 y1 x2 y2

Calculates the size in points of the smallest box which would completely enclose the current path. The coordinates of the lower left corner (x1 y1) and the upper right corner (x2 y2) are placed on the stack. The box is oriented with its sides parallel to the x and y axes. If rotations other than in units of 90 degrees have been used, the box may, depending upon its shape, be larger than anticipated.

See also: **clippath, flattenpath.**

pathforall

proc1 proc2 proc3 proc4 **pathforall** -

Executes one of the four given procedures for each part of the current path according to the operator which created each part of the path. Paths which contain segments created by the **charpath** operator cannot be processed by this operator.

Paths (other than those produced by **charpath**) may contain elements produced by the following operators: **moveto, lineto, curveto** and **closepath.** Other path creating operators (**rmoveto, rlineto, arc** etc) are first converted to the four operators listed above before **pathforall** is executed.

For each part of the current path, one of the given procedures is executed as follows:

moveto	place x y on stack; execute proc1
lineto	place x y on stack; execute proc2
curveto	place x1 y1 x2 y2 x3 y3 on stack; execute proc3
closepath	execute proc4

See also: **closepath, curveto, lineto, moveto.**

pop

object **pop** -

Removes the topmost object from the operand stack and discards it.

See also: **clear, cleartomark.**

print

string **print** -

Prints the given string to the current output file. This operator must not be confused with those operators which render marks onto the current page such as **show. print** allows programs to report on their progress to the user over a communications link.

See also =, ==, **flush, write.**

---

prompt

- prompt -

prompt is an internal POSTSCRIPT procedure. The procedure is executed in interactive mode when the previous command line has been interpreted and POSTSCRIPT is ready for another command line. The initial definition of **prompt** is {(PS>) print flush} although this may be changed by the user.

See also **echo, executive.**

---

pstack

lobject0... objectn **pstack** lobject0... objectn

Writes a text representation of every object on the operand stack to the current output file. This is a non-destructive operation, so the stack remains unchanged. The objects on the stack are dealt with topmost first, working down the stack.

See also: =, ==, **stack.**

---

put

array index object **put** -

dict key object **put** -

string index int **put** -

Places the topmost object on the stack into a specified position in an array, dictionary or string. In the case of an array or a string, the position for the new element is specified by index. Positions are counted from 0. String elements are given as an integer.

In the case of a dictionary, the specified key is given the new value. If key does not currently exist in that dictionary, a new entry is created with the given value. If the dictionary is already full an error is generated.

See also: **get, getinterval, putinterval.**

putinterval

array1 index array2 **putinterval** -

string1 index string2 **putinterval** -

Replaces the elements of array1 or string1 starting at element n (counting from 0) with the whole of array2 or string2 respectively.

See also: **get, getinterval, put.**

quit

- **quit** -

Halts operation of the interpreter. The precise effects of this operator are dependent on the implementation of POSTSCRIPT.

See also: **exit, start, stop.**

rand

- **rand** int

Returns to the stack a pseudo-random integer in the allowed POSTSCRIPT integer range. The state of the random number generator can be set with the operator **srand** and interrogated by **rrand**.

See also: **rrand, srand.**

rcheck

array **rcheck** bool

dict **rcheck** bool

file **rcheck** bool

ackedarray **rcheck** bool

string **rcheck** bool

Determines whether the value of the operand may be read by a POSTSCRIPT operator. If the operand's access level is read-only or unlimited, the boolean placed on the stack is true. Otherwise the boolean is false.

See also: **executeonly, noaccess, readonly, wcheck.**

rcurveto

x1 y1 x2 y2 x3 y3 **curveto** -

Appends a curve to the current path. The curve takes the form of a Bézier cubic section. The points x1 y1, x2 y2 and x3 y3 are considered as displacements from the current point in the graphics state, not as absolute coordinates. A full explanation of this geometric form is beyond the scope of this book, but see the operator **curveto** for fuller information. See also the section headed USING CURVETO in chapter 3.

See also: **arc, arcn, arcto, curveto, lineto, moveto.**

read

file **read**	(not end of file)	byte true
	(end of file)	false

Reads the next character from the named file. If a character is successfully read, the character and a true boolean are placed on the stack. If the end of file has been reached, however, the file is closed and a false boolean placed on the stack.

See also: **bytesavailable, readhexstring, readline, readstring.**

readhexstring

file string **readhexstring** substring bool

Reads a number of hexadecimal digits from the named file into the named string starting at position 0. The resulting full string is placed on the stack, followed by a true boolean. If the string is only partially filled before the end of file is reached, the substring used is placed on the stack followed by a false boolean.

Non-hexadecimal data is ignored by this operator, so white space characters may readily be used to format the data for easier human interpretation.

See also: **read, readline, readstring.**

readline

file string **readline** substring bool

Reads a line of data from the named file into the named string. The line of data in the file should be terminated with a newline character, but this character is not included in the resulting string. If a line of data is successfully read, the resulting string is placed on the stack, followed by a true boolean. If the string is only partially filled before the end of file is reached, the substring used is placed on the stack followed by a false boolean. If the string is completely filled before a newline is read, an error is generated.

See also: **read, readhexstring, readline.**

readonly

array **readonly** array

dict **readonly** dict

file **readonly** file

packedarray **readonly** packedarray

string **readonly** string

Reduces the access level of the operand to read-only. Access may never be restored to its previous level, so the value of the operand may not be modified after use of this operator.

See also: **executeonly, noaccess, rcheck, wcheck.**

readstring

file string **readstring** substring bool

Reads a number of characters from the named file into the named string starting at position 0. The resulting full string is placed on the stack, followed by a true boolean. If the string is only partially filled before the end of file is reached, the substring used is placed on the stack followed by a false boolean.

All characters (ASCII 0 to 255) are available to this operator, including white space characters such as newline and horizontal-tab.

See also: **read, readhexstring, readline.**

renderbands

proc **renderbands** -

Renders the contents of the current page for the currently installed output device, which was previously installed by the **banddevice** operator. The given procedure transfers the contents of the installed band buffer to the physical print device.

Only implementations of POSTSCRIPT which have the **banddevice** operator will have this operator and its use is dependent upon the hardware/software with which POSTSCRIPT is installed.

See also: **banddevice.**

repeat

int proc **repeat** -

The given procedure is executed as many times as indicated by the given integer. The integer must be positive, and is removed from the stack, along with the procedure, before the procedure is executed for the first time. If the integer is zero, the procedure is not executed at all.

See also: **exit, for, forall, loop, pathforall.**

resetfile

file **resetfile** -

Immediately discards any characters stored in buffers awaiting input or output to or from the named file. If the file is an input pile, all buffered data which has not yet been processed is discarded. If the file is an output file, all buffered data which has not yet been physically delivered is discarded.

See also: **closefile, file, flushfile.**

restore

VMstate **restore** -

Restores a previously saved 'snapshot' of virtual memory. The snapshot, generated by a previous use of the **save** operator, must be on top of the operand stack. The saved VM state may be assigned to a variable like any other POSTSCRIPT object.

See also: **grestoreall, save, vmstatus.**

---
reversepath

- reversepath -

Replaces the current path with one with the same form, but whose elements were appended in the reverse order and the reverse direction. Use of this operator does not alter the order of the subpaths within the current path.

See also: **clip, currentpoint, eoclip, eofill, fill.**

---
rlineto
---

x y **rlineto** -

Removes the two operands from the stack and appends a straight line segment to the the current path. The line joins the current point and a point offset from the current point by x and y respectively.

See also: **arc, arcn, closepath, curveto, lineto, moveto, rmoveto.**

---
rmoveto
---

x y **rmoveto** -

Moves the current point across and up by x and y respectively, starting a new sub-path of the current path in the graphics state.

See also: **arc, arcn, closepath, curveto, lineto, moveto, rlineto.**

---
roll

Removes the top two operands from the stack and performs a circular shift of the n topmost objects on the stack by p positions. If p is positive, the shift is upwards on the stack; if p is negative, the shift is downwards. Both n and p must be integers and n must be positive. For example:

(one)(two)(three)(four) 5 1 **roll** > (four)(one)(two)(three)

(one)(two)(three)(four) 5 -1 **roll** > (two)(three)(four)(one)

See also: **copy, dup, exch, index, pop.**

rotate

angle **rotate** -

angle matrix **rotate** matrix

With no matrix operand, this operator builds a matrix as follows:

$$\begin{matrix} \cos O & \sin O & 0 \\ -\sin O & \cos O & 0 \\ 0 & 0 & 1 \end{matrix}$$

where O is the given angle (in degrees). This matrix is then concatenated with the current transformation matrix (CTM). This has the effect of rotating the coordinate system of the current page anticlockwise about the origin by the given number of degrees.

With a matrix operand, the value of the given matrix is replaced by the matrix above. The modified matrix is then placed on the operand stack. This has no effect on the coordinate system.

See also **concat, matrix, scale, translate.**

round

num1 **round** num2

Returns the nearest integer value to num1. The returned value is a real, not an integer. If the operand is equally distanced from two integers, the greater value is returned.

See also: **ceiling, cvi, floor, truncate.**

rrand

rrand int

Returns an integer which, when used as an operand to **srand**, will set the random number generator to a specific point in its sequence. This allows a sequence of pseudo-random numbers to be repeated.

See also: **rand, srand.**

---

run

string **run** -

Executes the contents of the named file, which must contain a POSTSCRIPT program.

See also: **cvx, exec, file.**

---

save

- **save** -

Places a 'snapshot' of the virtual memory on the operand stack. This snapshot may later be restored by use of the **restore** operator. This operator also saves the current graphics state on the graphics state stack in the same manner as **gsave**. The saved graphics state is restored by use of **restore** and **grestoreall.**

See also: **grestoreall, gsave, restore, vmstatus.**

---

scale

num1 num2 **scale** -

num1 num2 matrix **scale** matrix

With no matrix operand, this operator builds a matrix as follows:

num1	0	0
0	num2	0
0	0	1

and concatenates it with the current transformation matrix (CTM). This has the effect of scaling the coordinate system of the current page by num1 times in the x direction and num2 times in the y direction.

With a matrix operand, the value of the given matrix is replaced by the matrix above. The modified matrix is then placed on the operand stack. This has no effect on the coordinate system.

See also: **concat, matrix, rotate, scale.**

scalefont

font1 scale **scalefont** font2

Scales the named font by the given scale factor is both the x any y directions and places the new scaled font on the operand stack. This may then be set to the current font using **setfont.**

See also: **findfont, makefont, setfont.**

search

| string1 string2 **search** | (if found) | post match pre true |
| string1 string2 **search** | (if not found) | string1 false |

Searches string1 for the first occurrence of string2. If string2 is found, the part of string1 following the match is placed on the stack, followed by the matching section (string2), the part of string1 preceding the match and a true boolean. If string2 is not found within string1, string1 is placed on the stack, followed by a false boolean.

See also: **anchorsearch, token.**

setcachedevice

widx widy x1 y1 x2 y2 **setcachedevice** -

Passes information regarding a character being built with the **BuildChar** operator to the POSTSCRIPT font processor. The operands represent the x and y 'widths' of the current character and the bounding box of the current character (x1 y1 is the lower left of the bounding box and x2 y2 the upper right).

See also: **BuildChar, cachestatus, setcachelimit, setcharwidth.**

setcachelimit

num **setcachelimit** -

Sets the maximum number of bytes which the bit image for any cached character may occupy. If a character is built (with **BuildChar**) which uses more than this number of bytes, then the character is not cached, but recalculated each time it is used after the font is built. The value of num affects the maximum number of characters which may be cached. The limit for num is device dependent.

See also: **BuildChar, cachestatus, setcachedevice.**

setcacheparams

mark int1 int2 **setcacheparams** -

Sets the maximum number of bytes which the bit image for any cached character may occupy (int2) and the threshold below which the character data is compressed for storage (int1). Compressed characters are de-compressed each time they are used. If int1 is zero, all characters are compressed, increasing the maximum number of characters which may be cached. If int1 is greater than or equal to int2, compression is disabled.

The reason for the **mark** (which along with the two operands is removed from the stack after execution of **setcacheparams**) is that different versions of POSTSCRIPT may require different numbers of operands. If more operands than required are supplied, the topmost operands are used and the lower ones discarded along with the **mark**. If less operands than required are supplied, default values are inserted between the **mark** and the first operand above the **mark**.

See also: **currentcacheparams, mark, setcachedevice, setcachelimit.**

setcharwidth

x y **setcharwidth** -

Sets the x and y 'width' of the character being built with **BuildChar**. This operator also specifies that the character is not to be cached, but recalculated each time it is needed. This allows the character description to use any of the operators which set color or gray shade; these are unavailable to cached characters.

See also: **setcachedevice.**

setdash

array offset **setdash** -

Sets the pattern of dashes of lines produced in the graphics state. The array, whose elements must be positive and not all zero, represents the 'on' and 'off' parts of the line, the pattern repeating along the length of the line. The offset specifies the number of 'on' or 'off' units into the pattern that the pattern starts at the beginning of the first line produced. The pattern restarts at the beginning of each subpath.

If the given array is empty, the pattern produced is an unbroken line.

See also: currentdash.

setflat

num setflat -

Sets the 'flatness' of curves produced in the graphics state. Curves are rendered onto the current page as an approximation made up from numerous straight lines. A low value of num (minimum 0.2) will produce a very smooth curve at the expense of processing time. A higher value of num (maximum 100) will produce a less accurate line in less time.

This operator affects the shape of paths, therefore the effects of stroke and the clip and fill operators will all change according to its use. The default setflat value is device dependent.

See also: clip, currentflat, fill, flattenpath, stroke.

setfont

font setfont

Sets the given font to be the current font for all subsequent font operations.

See also: currentfont, findfont, makefont, scalefont.

setgray

num setgray -

Sets the shade of gray used for all subsequent print operations such as show, stroke and fill. The value of num must lie between 0 (black) and 1 (white).

See also: currentgray, sethsbcolor, setrgbcolour.

sethsbcolor

hue saturation brightness sethsbcolor -

Sets the current color in the graphics state for all subsequent print operations such as show, stroke and fill. Values of the three operands must lie in the range 0 to 1.

See also: **currentgray, currenthsbcolor, setrgbcolor.**

setlinecap

int **setlinecap** -

Sets the shape of the ends of lines and arcs produced in the graphics state. The value of int must be in the range 0 to 2 as follows:

0   square line end at the end of the path
1   semicircular line end centered on the centre of the line at the end of the path
2   square line end projecting beyond the end of the line by half the width of the line.

See also: **currentlinecap, setlinejoin, setdash, stroke.**

setlinejoin

int **setlinejoin** -

Sets the shape of the joins between lines and arcs produced in the graphics state. The value of int must be in the range 0 to 2 as follows:

0   outer edges of lines mitered together to a point
1   outer edges of lines rounded together, centered on the join of the two meeting segments of the path
2   lines drawn with butt end caps (**setlinecap** with operand 0) and the resulting notch filled to produce a chamfered corner.

See also: **currentlinejoin, setlinecap, setmiterlimit, stroke.**

setlinewidth

num **setlinewidth** -

Sets the width of lines and arcs produced in the graphics state. The lines produced have as their centre, the actual position of the path, therefore part of the line projects out on either side of the path by half of the current line width.

Note that if the x and y axes have been scaled by different factors, the thickness of lines will vary according to their position relative to the x and y axes.

A value of num of 0 is allowed, but some output devices may either produce a line which is difficult to see or not be able to render such a fine line. A value of 0 sets the line width to one device pixel.

See also: **currentlinewidth, stroke.**

setmatrix

matrix **setmatrix** -

Makes the given matrix the current transformation matrix (CTM) in the graphics state.

See also: **concat, currentmatrix, defaultmatrix, initmatrix, rotate, scale, translate.**

setmiterlimit

num **setmiterlimit** -

Sets a limit on the projecting outer corner of line joins in the graphics state after the use of **setlinejoin** with an operand of 0. The value of num, which must be greater than or equal to 1, refers to the ratio between the length of the miter (distance between the inside and outside corners of the join) and the line width according to the formula:

$$\text{miter length / line width} = 1 / \sin (\text{inside join angle} / 2)$$

If the ratio between the miter length and the line width exceeds the given value of num, the line join is treated as if it were produced after the use of **setlinejoin** with an operand of 2 (chamfered corner).

The default value of the miter limit is 10, which truncates miters formed between lines joining at angles less than 11 degrees.

See also: **currentmiterlimit, setlinejoin, stroke.**

setpacking

bool **setpacking** -

Enables or disables packing of executable arrays subsequently created. A true boolean enables array packing; a false boolean disables array packing.

See also: **currentpacking, packedarray.**

---

setrgbcolor

red green blue **setrgbcolor** -

Sets the current color in the graphics state for all subsequent print operations such as **show, stroke** and **fill.** Values of the three operands must lie in the range 0 to 1.

See also: **currentgray, currentrgbcolor, sethsbcolor.**

---

setscreen

freq angle proc **setscreen** -

Define a halftone screen for use in the graphics state. The first operand, freq, defines the frequency (halftone cells per inch) of the screen; the second operand, angle, sets the angle of the halftone and the procedure proc specifies the way the pixels within a cell are arranged to produce any shade of gray.

All POSTSCRIPT output devices set up a default halftone screen during their initialisation which is designed to avoid the occurrence of moire patterns.

See also **currentscreen, settransfer.**

---

settransfer

proc **settransfer** -

Uses the given procedure to map the currently set gray value (**currentgray**) to the output device.

See also: **currenttransfer, setscreen.**

---

show

string **show** -

Renders the given string onto the current page, using the current font and gray level, starting at the current point.

See also: **ashow, awidthshow, charpath, findfont, kshow, moveto, scalefont, setfont, widthshow.**

---

showpage

- showpage -

Commands the physical print device to print the current page. More than one copy can be produced by the operators **copypage** and **showpage** by changing the default setting of the POSTSCRIPT variable #copies. For example, to issue 10 copies of the current page, include in your program the line:

```
/#copies 10 def
```

See also: **copypage, erasepage.**

---

sin

angle **sin** num

Removes the top number from the stack and returns to the stack the natural sine of that angle. The angle is taken to be a number of degrees.

See also: **cos, atan.**

---

sqrt

num1 **sqrt** num2

Removes num1 from the stack and returns to the stack its square root. The value of num1 must be positive. The result is a real number.

See also: **exp.**

---

srand

int **srand** -

Seeds the pseudo-random number generator with the given integer. This allows the same set of random numbers to be generated more than once by re-seeding with a particular integer.

See also: **rand, rrand.**

---

stack

lobj1... objn **stack** lobj1... objn

Sends a text representation of the entire contents of the stack to the current output file, leaving the stack unchanged. The topmost object on the stack is sent first, the bottommost last. This operator repeatedly uses the = operator to send the representations of stacked objects.

See also: =, ==, **count, pstack.**

StandardEncoding

- StandardEncoding array

(Note that the capital letters are significant). Places on the stack a 256 element array containing character names indexed by the character codes in the standard POSTSCRIPT character set. The values of the character names are the characters themselves.

See also: **array.**

start

- start -

An internal POSTSCRIPT procedure which is executed when the POSTSCRIPT interpreter is initialised. The actions performed by **start** are device dependent.

See also: **quit.**

status

file **status** bool

Returns to the stack a true boolean if the named file is open, a false boolean otherwise.

See also: **closefile, file.**

stop

- stop -

Halts execution of the executable used as an operand to the operator **stopped**, clears the execution stack down to the **stopped** operator and places a true boolean on the operand stack. Execution continues at the point immediately following the **stopped** operator.

See also: **exit, stopped.**

stopped

> obj **stopped** bool

Executes the given object and, if no **stop** operator is encountered during execution of the operand, places a false boolean on the operand stack. The use of this operator in conjunction with the **stop** operator allows errors to be trapped and handled by the user.

See also: **exit, stop.**

store

> key value **store** -

Searches the dictionaries on the dictionary stack in turn, starting with the current (topmost) dictionary, for the given key. If the key is found in one of the dictionaries, its value is replaced with the given value. If the given key is not found in any of the dictionaries on the dictionary stack, a new entry is created for the key/value pair in the current dictionary. In the latter case, if the current dictionary is full an error is generated.

See also: **def, put, where.**

string

> int **string** string

Creates a string object of the length specified by the given integer and places the blank string on the stack.

See also: **array, cvs, length, stringwidth, type.**

stringwidth

> string **stringwidth** num1 num2

Calculates the change in position of the current point effected by the showing of the given string using the current font. The change in x position is given by num1 and the change in the y position by num2.

See also: **setfont, show.**

---

stroke

- stroke -

renders a line onto the current page taking the form of the current path and in the current color at the current line width. This operator also performs a **newpath** after rendering the current path.

See also: **setlinecap, setdash, setlinejoin, setlinewidth, setmiterlimit.**

---

strokepath

- strokepath -

Replaces the current path with one which would completely enclose the current path if the **stroke** operator were applied to that path. The resulting path may be clipped of filled, but may not always be stroked.

See also: **clip, charpath, fill, pathbbox, stroke.**

---

sub

num1 num2 sub num3

Removes the two operands from the stack and subtracts num2 from num1. The result, num3, is placed on the stack. If both operands are integers and their difference is within the range for integers allowed by POSTSCRIPT, the result is also an integer. Otherwise the result is a real number.

See also: **add, div, idiv, mod, mul.**

---

systemdict

- systemdict -

Places the dictionary **systemdict** on the operator stack. This is not an operator, simply the name of the dictionary **systemdict.**

See also: **dict, errordict, userdict.**

---

token

file **token**	(if found)	object true
file **token**	(if not found)	false
string1 **token**	(if found)	string2 object true
string1 **token**	(if not found)	false

Reads characters from the given file or string, interpreting them as a POSTSCRIPT program, until a complete object has been scanned and constructed. In the case of a file, the scanned object is placed on the operand stack followed by a true boolean. If the end of file is reached before a full object is read, the file is closed and a false boolean placed on the operand stack.

In the case of a string, the part of the given string not used to construct the object is placed on the operand stack, followed by the object and a true boolean. If the end of the string is reached before a full object is read, a false boolean is placed on the operand stack.

The resulting object in each case is a full POSTSCRIPT object of any type, but is not immediately executed, just placed on the operand stack.

See also: **anchorsearch, read, search.**

---

transform

x y **transform** x' y'

x y matrix **transform** x' y'

If no matrix is supplied, the user space coordinates x and y are transformed by the current transformation matrix (CTM) to produce the point x' y'. These coordinates are returned to the stack.

If a matrix is supplied, the user space coordinates x and y are transformed by the given to produce the point x' y'. These coordinates are returned to the stack.

See also: **itransform, dtransform, idtransform, matrix.**

translate

distx disty **translate** -

With no matrix operand, this operator builds a matrix as follows:

distx	0	0
0	disty	0
0	0	1

and concatenates it with the current transformation matrix (CTM). This has the effect of moving the origin of the coordinate system of the current page by distx points in the x direction and disty points in the y direction.

With a matrix operand, the value of the given matrix is replaced by the matrix above. The modified matrix is then placed on the operand stack. This has no effect on the coordinate system.

See also: **concat, matrix, rotate, scale, setmatrix.**

true

- **true** true

Places a true boolean on the operand stack. This object can then be tested by various POSTSCRIPT operators.

See also: **and, false, not, or, xor.**

truncate

num1 **truncate** num2

Removes any fractional part of num1, which is then returned to the stack as num2. The returned number is the same type as the operand num1.

See also: **ceiling, cvi, floor, round.**

type

obj **type** name

Returns an executable name object matching the type of operand. For example, a string operand would result in the name **stringtype** being returned to the stack.

---

userdict

- **userdict** dict

Places the dictionary object **userdict** on the operand stack. This is not an operator, simply the name of the dictionary **userdict**.

See also: **dict, errordict, systemdict.**

---

usertime

- **usertime** int

Returns to the stack the value of an internal counter which indicates the number of milliseconds the POSTSCRIPT interpreter has been running. The returned value has no relevance to the actual time of day. The accuracy of the counter is device dependent.

---

version

- **version** string

Returns to the stack a string representing the version number of the POSTSCRIPT interpreter being used.

---

vmstatus

- **vmstatus** saves used max

Returns to the stack the number of currently unrestored saves, the amount of virtual memory currently used and the maximum amount of virtual memory. The virtual memory is described in units of 8 bytes. The maximum amount of memory is not an absolute, different implementations of POSTSCRIPT may have different amounts of virtual memory and, in some implementations, this figure may be increased according to need.

See also: **restore, save.**

---

wcheck

array **wcheck** bool

dict **wcheck** bool

file **wcheck** bool

packedarray **wcheck** false

string **wcheck** bool

Determines whether a new value may be written to the operand. A true boolean is returned if the access of the given object is unlimited; a false boolean otherwise. Packed arrays can never have unlimited access, so a false boolean is always returned when the operand is a packed array.

See also: **executeonly, noaccess, rcheck, readonly.**

where

key **where** (if found)   dict true

key **where** (if not found)   false

Searches the dictionaries on the dictionary stack, starting with the topmost, for the given key. If the key is found in any of the dictionaries, that dictionary is placed on the operand stack, followed by a boolean true. If the key is not found in any of the dictionaries, a boolean false is placed on the stack.

See also: **get, known, load.**

widthshow

distx disty char string **widthshow** -

Prints the characters in the given string, adding the values of distx and disty to the x and y positions respectively after printing each occurrence of the given character. The character should be specified by its ASCII code (an integer in the range 0 to 255).

See also: **ashow, awidthshow, kshow, show, stringwidth.**

write

file int **write** -

Appends a single character to a named output file. The character is specified by its ASCII code (an integer in the range 0 to 255).

See also: **file, read, readhexstring, writehexstring, writestring.**

writehexstring

file string **writehexstring** -

Appends the ASCII codes of all the characters in the given string to the given file in two-digit hexadecimal format.

See also: **file, read, readhexstring, write, writestring.**

writestring

file string **writestring** -

Appends the value of the given string to the given output file.

See also: **file, read, readhexstring, write, writehexstring.**

xcheck

object **xcheck** bool

Determines whether the given object is executable or literal. If the object is executable, a true boolean is returned to the stack, otherwise a false boolean is returned to the stack.

See also: **cvlit, cvx.**

xor

bool1 bool2 **xor** bool3

int1 int2 **xor** int3

If the operands are booleans, the result of a logical 'exclusive or' of the two operands is returned to the stack. If the operands are integers, the bitwise 'exclusive or' of their binary representations is returned to the stack.

See also: **and, false, not, or, true.**

APPENDIX A

POSTSCRIPT TYPESETTING

The introduction to this book and chapter 1 both mention the possibilities of POSTSCRIPT typesetting. This means producing reproduction quality artwork from a POSTSCRIPT file. The file may be produced as output from one of the growing number of desk-top-publishing programs, a drawing package, a CAD package, or the file may be a POSTSCRIPT program written by yourself to manipulate text or graphics.

Your POSTSCRIPT file, instead of being printed out by a laser printer costing three or four thousand pounds, is printed out by a typesetting machine which can cost around a hundred thousand pounds. The output will be very much the same; text is printed at the same size and in the same place and graphics are produced in exactly the same way on both machines. The difference is in the resolution at which the printers operate.

Most desk-top laser printers operate at a resolution of 300 dots per inch; a typesetting machine will produce output at between 1200 and 2400 dots per inch. That quality of output is sufficient for all but the largest of display work (billboards and the like).

More and more typesetting companies are adding the equipment to their typesetting operations to allow them to accept POSTSCRIPT files for output. Charges are based on either each page of output or each minute of machine time. In the latter case, complex graphics, for example, will cost more than plain text.

POSTSCRIPT FILE CONVENTIONS

The originators of POSTSCRIPT, Adobe Systems Incorporated, have specified a series of conventions for the header and trailer of POSTSCRIPT files. These allow POSTSCRIPT files to be easily identified as such and to be handled properly by some operating systems. The following is an example of a POSTSCRIPT program which has the recommended header and trailer:

```
%!PS-Adobe-1.0
%%Title: Freehand POSTSCRIPT Document
%%Creator: BARRY THOMAS
%%Pages: (atend)
%%BoundingBox: 0 0 595 841
%%EndComments

300 420 100 0 360 arc          % draw circle
stroke                         % stroke onto page
showpage                       % print it

%%Trailer
%%Pages: 1
%%EOF
```

The most important part of the header is the first two characters. These, (%!), identify this as a POSTSCRIPT file to certain systems, for example, UNIX. The next three lines of the header give the file title, its creator (this might be Ventura Publisher or Aldus Pagemaker, for example) and the number of pages. The last of these, in this example, indicates that the number of pages is to be found at the end of the POSTSCRIPT file.

The next line gives the bottom left and top right coordinates of a box which would completely enclose each page of the output of the program. The next line indicates the end of the header comments. The next part of the file is the POSTSCRIPT program itself. In this case, the program simply draws a circle at the centre of an A4 page.

The trailer starts with a line which indicates that the rest of the file is trailer text. The next line gives the number of pages produced by the file and the last line the end of file indicator (EOF). The last character of a POSTSCRIPT file should be ASCII 04x (04 decimal).

For full details of the POSTSCRIPT file conventions, refer to the POSTSCRIPT Language Reference Manual, published by Addison Wesley Publishing Company.

TYPESETTER OUTPUT

Having prepared your POSTSCRIPT files, give a copy on a disk to the typesetting company and they do the rest. Most will take disks in IBM PC 5.25 or 3.5 format or Apple Macintosh format.

The following page shows how a POSTSCRIPT file appears when printed on a 300 dpi laser printer (like the rest of this book) in comparison with the output from a typesetting machine.

The POSTSCRIPT programs for this page were written by the author on an IBM PC compatible using the non-document mode of Wordstar. The files were output on a QMS PS 800+ laser printer and on a Linotronic typesetting machine with a Raster Image Processor (RIP). The company which produced the Linotronic output is Lotus Reprographic Services Ltd, London, W6.

Laser printer output

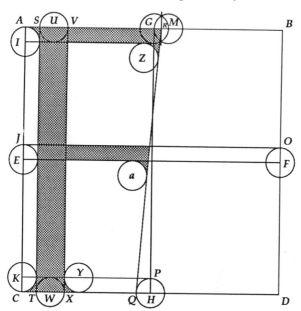

Linotronic output

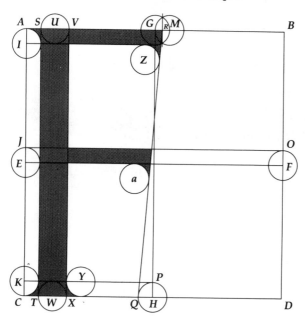

APPENDIX B

EXECUTIVE MODE

When writing and testing your own POSTSCRIPT programs, it is possible to send the programs as complete files straight to your POSTSCRIPT printer by using some form of two-way communications software. In the event of a fatal error, the type of error which caused the program to halt is reported back to the current output file, i.e., by default back over the communication line.

You can then see the reason for the crash and attempt to correct the problem. Appendix D lists the possible errors and their meanings. Error messages sent by the POSTSCRIPT interpreter also contain the line:

```
%%[ Flushing: rest of job (to end-of-file) will be
ignored ]%%
```

This means that, even if you continue sending program lines to the printer, all further commands will be ignored up until the end-of-file (EOF) marker. The POSTSCRIPT EOF is a CONTROL D character (ASCII 04). After receiving a CONTROL D, the POSTSCRIPT interpreter is then ready to continue processing your programs.

Another way to test programs and parts of programs is to send them, operator by operator or line by line in interactive mode. This is known as **executive** mode.

STARTING EXECUTIVE

Before starting **executive** mode, check that the device is ready by sending a control T character (hold down CONTROL and press T). If the POSTSCRIPT printer is ready, it will send back a message like:

```
%%[ status: idle ]%%
```

This shows that the printer is in idle mode.

137

To enter **executive** mode, simply type **executive** and press [RETURN]. The printer will then echo back all information sent to it so your communications software should be set to FULL DUPLEX.

Your screen should show the **executive** start-up message:

```
PostScript(r) Version XX.X
Copyright (c) 1986 Adobe Systems Incorporated.
PS>
```

Now if you send a CONTROL T to determine the printer status, you will receive the message:

```
%%[ status: waiting; source: serial 25 ]%%
```

This shows that the printer is in **executive** mode, waiting for input, and that this particular printer has a selection of interfaces, but the current one is 25 pin serial.

There now follows a transcription of an **executive** session, during which a couple of arithmetic operations are performed followed by the selection and scaling of a typeface and the printing of a text string. Note the PS> prompt offered by the printer at the start of each line of my input. Information reported back from the printer (in response to = and **pstack**) are shown in bold type:

```
PS>4 5 add
PS>=
9
PS>4 dup mul
PS>=
16
PS>100 100 translate
PS>0 0 moveto
PS>/Times-Roman findfont
PS>24 scalefont
PS>setfont
PS>(Barry Thomas)
PS>pstack
(Barry Thomas)
PS>show
PS>showpage
PS>
```

At this point, the printer issues a page showing the text string Barry Thomas.

ERRORS

If you issue any commands during an **executive** session which the printer cannot interpret successfully, an error message will be reported back. For example, the message:

```
%%[ Error: nocurrentpoint; OffendingCommand: show ]%%
```

indicates that a **show** was effected when no current point had been defined. At this point you can still continue sending commands. The interpreter is still operating and will effect all correctly stated commands and operators.

Note that when in **executive** mode, some operators will have an immediate effect and the PS> prompt will be redisplayed instantly. Other operators, especially those concerned with font selection and graphics will take longer. The PS> prompt will then be redisplayed and you can continue sending commands.

RECURSIVE EXECUTIVE

Note also that it is possible to enter **executive** mode recursively. When in **executive** mode, the prompt returned after each line is PS>. Should you now issue the **executive** command again, the prompt will be PS>>, the number of arrows showing the depth of recursion. To escape from each level of **executive**, send a CONTROL D character. After each CONTROL D, the PS> prompt will be displayed with the appropriate number of arrows - one less with each CONTROL D.

CONTROL COMMANDS

The following control keys have the effects shown:

CTRL C (ASCII 03)	cancel current command line
CTRL D (ASCII 04)	end-of-file (device 'reset' and exit executive)
CTRL I (ASCII 09)	operator delimiter
CTRL T (ASCII 20)	status enquiry

APPENDIX C

POSTSCRIPT LIMITS

Like other programming languages, POSTSCRIPT limits the length of strings, the size of integers and so on. This appendix lists the basic implementation limits of the language. Some of these limits, for example, the maximum number of files open, may be greater on certain implementations.

array	max objects in an array: 65535
dash	max elements in a dash pattern: 8 (see **setdash**)
dict stack	max number of objects: 20
exec stack	max number of objects: 250
file	max number of open files: 6 (device dependent)
FontDirectory	max number of currently defined fonts: 100
gsave level	max number of unrestored **gsaves**: 31
integer	allowed integer range: -2^{31} to $2^{31} -1$
interpreter level	max recursive invocations of POSTSCRIPT: 10
name	max name length: 128
operand stack	max number of objects: 500
path	max number of points in all active or saved paths: 1500
procedure	max objects in definition
real	allowed real number range: $\pm 10^{38}$ to 8 significant decimal digits (approximately)
save level	max number of unrestored **saves**: 15
string	max string length: 65535
userdict	max capacity: 200
VM	max number of bytes virtual memory: 240000

APPENDIX D

ERROR MESSAGES

This appendix lists errors which may occur during the execution of a POSTSCRIPT program. Other, device-dependent, errors may occur, such as when a printer's paper tray is empty or the device is non-operational for some other reason.

Error messages reported back take the following form:

```
%%[ Error: nocurrentpoint; OffendingCommand: show ]%%
```

The message shows that the error was **nocurrentpoint** and that the offending command was the **show** operator. In other words, the program attempted to **show** a piece of text when no current point had been defined.

The following error messages may be issued:

dictfull	no more room in current dictionary
dictstackoverflow	too many **begins** used
dictstackunderflow	too many **ends** used
execstackoverflow	**exec** nesting too deep
handleerror	used when reporting errors
interrupt	external interrupt
invalidaccess	access of array, packed array etc not allowed
invalidexit	**exit** operator is not inside a loop
invalidfileaccess	file access not allowed
invalidfont	font or dictionary name not allowed
invalidrestore	restore after other objects created and stacked
ioerror	input/output (communications) error
limitcheck	limits of implementation exceeded
nocurrentpoint	no current point defined
rangecheck	limits for operand exceeded
stackoverflow	operand stack overflow
stackunderflow	operand stack underflow

syntaxerror	program contains syntax error
timeout	wait time limit exceeded
typecheck	wrong operand type given
undefined	name (proc or variable) not currently defined
undefinedfilename	file not found
undefinedresult	result exceeds implementation limits or meaningless
unmatchedmark	expected **mark** not found on stack
unregistered	internal error
VMerror	out of memory

INDEX